T0042626

SELP-
HeLF

Gallery Books

New York

London

Toronto

Sydney

New Delhi

SELP-HELF

by

Miranda Sings

Gallery Books
An Imprint of Simon & Schuster, Inc.
1230 Avenue of the Americas
New York, NY 10020

Copyright © 2015 by Miranda Sings, Inc.

All rights reserved, including the right to reproduce this book or portions thereof in any form whatsoever. For information address Gallery Books Subsidiary Rights Department, 1230 Avenue of the Americas, New York, NY 10020

First Gallery Books trade paperback edition June 2019

GALLERY BOOKS and colophon are registered trademarks of Simon & Schuster, Inc.

For information about special discounts for bulk purchases, please contact Simon & Schuster Special Sales at 1-866-506-1949 or business@simonandschuster.com

The Simon & Schuster Speakers Bureau can bring authors to your live event. For more information or to book an event contact the Simon & Schuster Speakers Bureau at 1-866-248-3049 or visit our website at www.simonspeakers.com.

Manufactured in the United States of America

1 3 5 7 9 10 8 6 4 2

Library of Congress Cataloging-in-Publication Data is available.

ISBN 978-1-5011-1794-7 (hardcover)
ISBN 978-1-5011-1795-4
ISBN 978-1-5011-1797-8 (ebook)

Photo of Miranda on pg. 170 courtesy of James Shubinski.

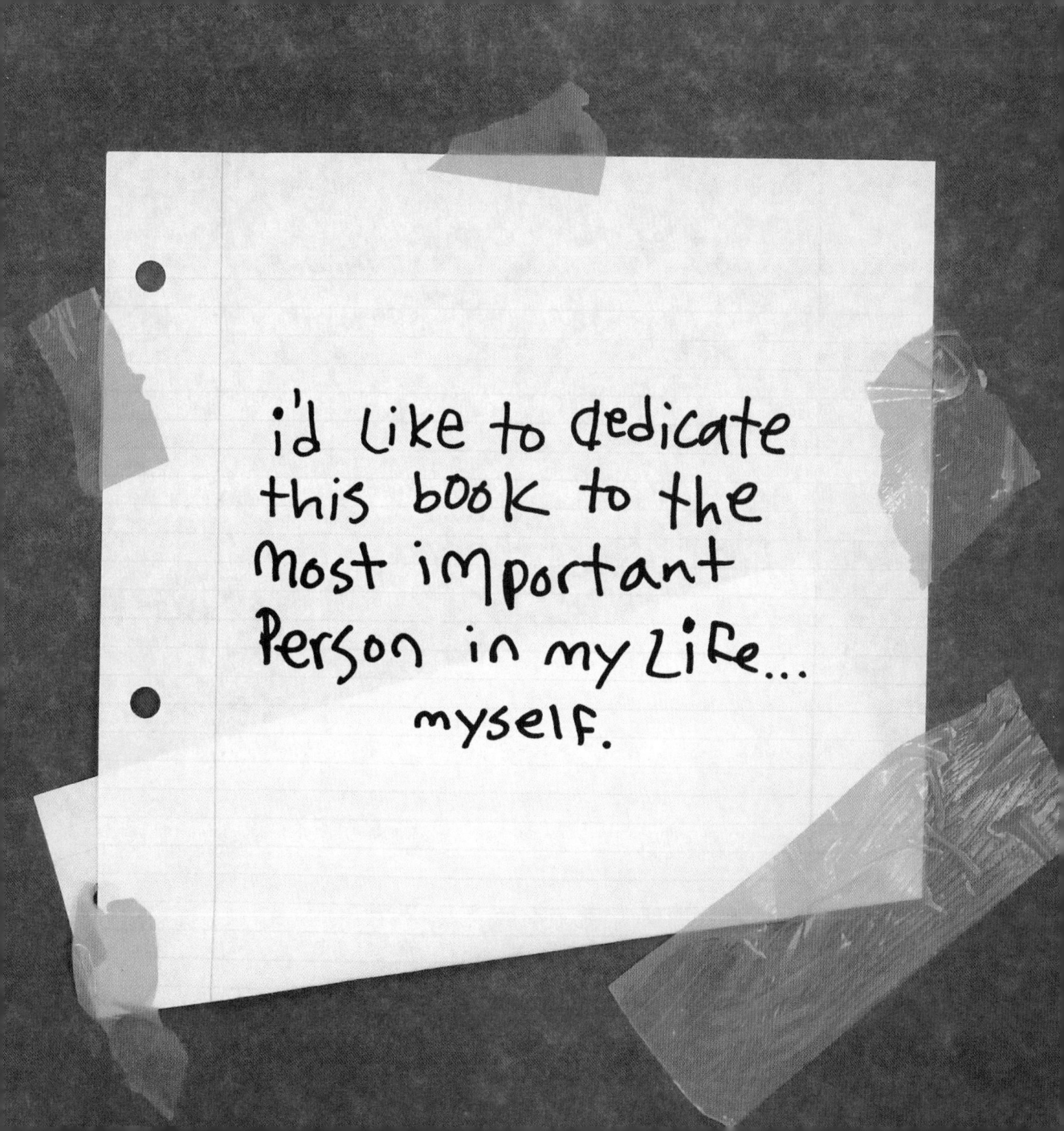
i'd like to dedicate
this book to the
most important
person in my life...
myself.

DISCLAMER

This book has a lot of cutouts and activities wear you draw in the book. So you need to get a back up book. Go Buy another one rite now so you can cut this 1 up and drawl in it and have a extra 1 that is perfeck.

Also, im NOT responsible 4 injury to person or Property as a result of using my good advice in this book. So dont sue me cuz im Not that type of girl.

Table of Contents

Table of Contents.....now
Introducshon.....viii
Love.....3
Talent.....27
Fashon.....45
Career.....73
Finances.....89
Smart.....111
Innernet.....113
Health.....139
Self Esteem.....167
Kids.....187
Life Haks.....209
Concluchin.....231

INTRODUCTION

welcome to my selp helf book. in this book I will supply you with the best advice in the world on becoming a better person. By the end of this book your love life, career, self esteem, finances, health, etc will all be perfect. Your welcome.

Being Born

ABOUT ME

i was borned on December 24, one day bef Jesus so you know, just saying. Right away they knew i was destined for grateness because i beat the placenta out of the tookie.

As I grew older my fans realized my many talents such as acting, modeling, book writing and such as.

Dont belive me? Just look at this modeling pic from when i was a baby.

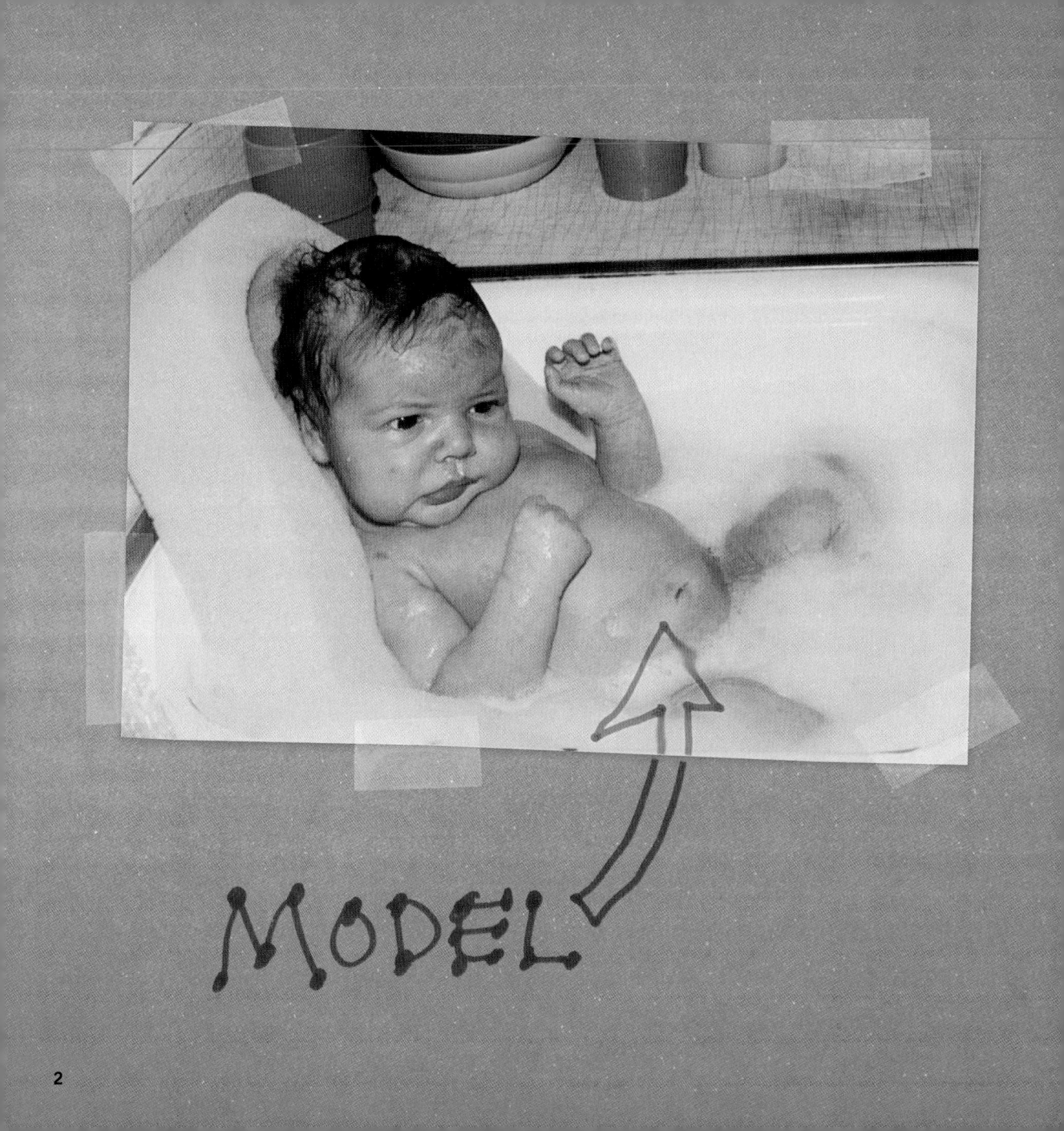
MODEL

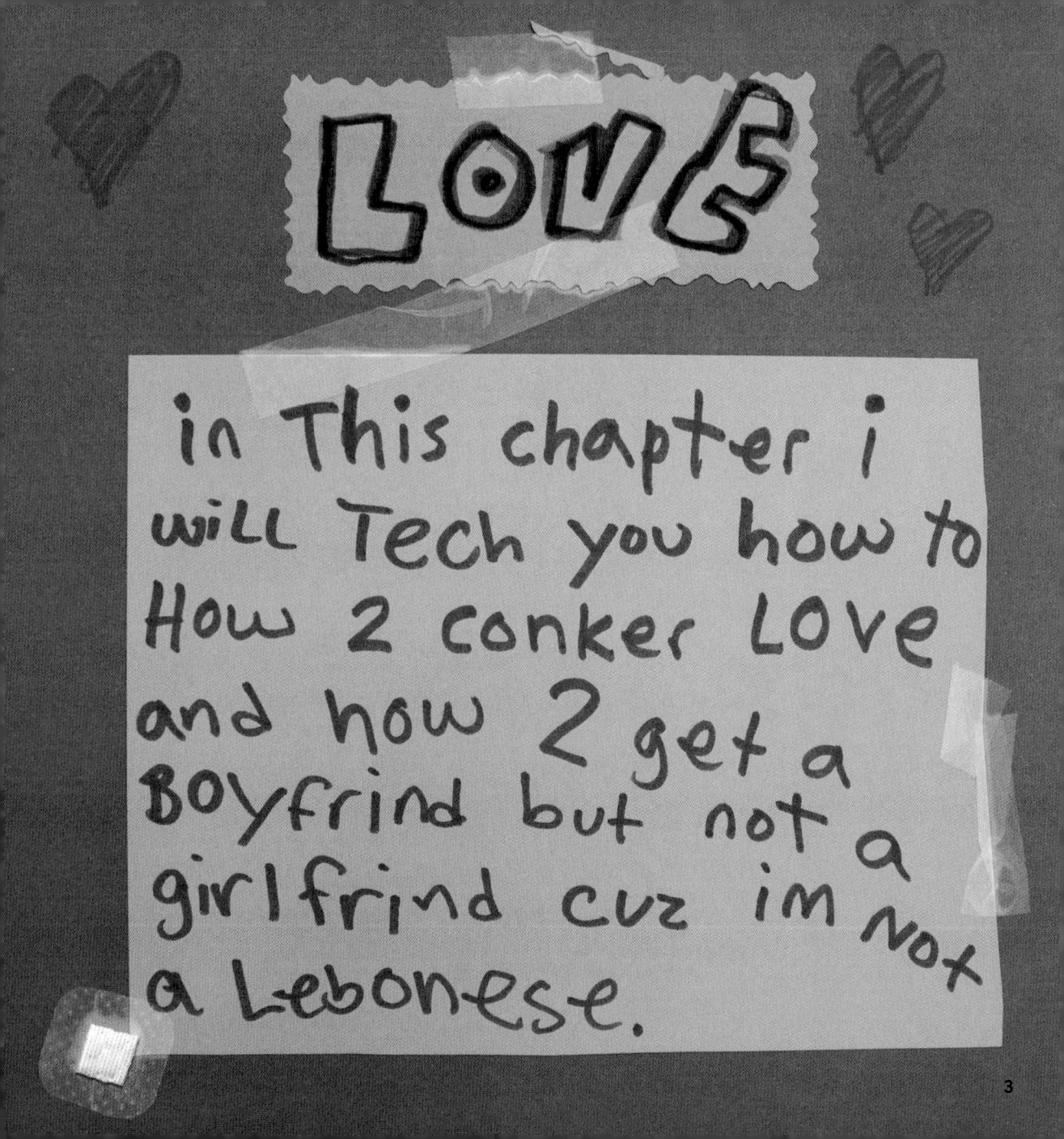

LOVE

in This chapter i will Tech you how to How 2 conker LOVE and how 2 get a Boyfrind but not a girlfrind cuz im Not a Lebonese.

Qualities to Look For.

Attracive

Pretty

Hairs

Rich

This

Famus

Qualities
To Have.
cute
Bootiful
Sensual
Pritty
Atractive

LOVE LANGUAGES
Every1 shows Love through 1 of the 5 Love languages. Hear R the 5 languages and how they R used.
EYE LANGUAGE
i see you
yeh rite
BODY LANGUAGE
Come here
COME HERE

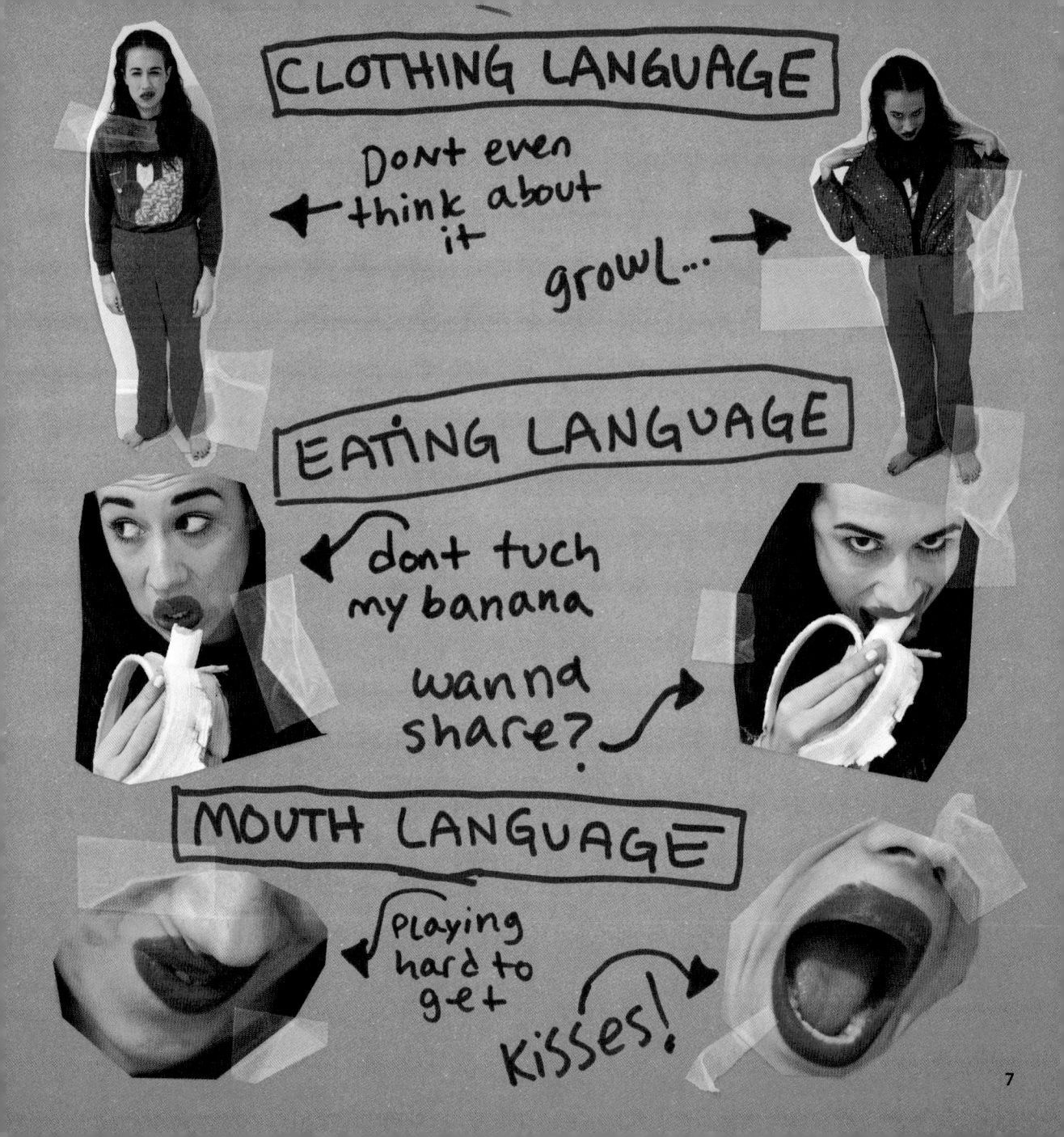
CLOTHING LANGUAGE
Dont even think about it
growl...
EATING LANGUAGE
dont tuch my banana
wanna share?
MOUTH LANGUAGE
playing hard to get
Kisses!

Get A BoyFrind Kit
Binoculars
Perfume
Black clothes
Handcuffs
Rubber gloves
Camera with Night vision
FLashlite

GET A GIRLFRIEND KIT
$ $ Have money. $ $
¢ ¢

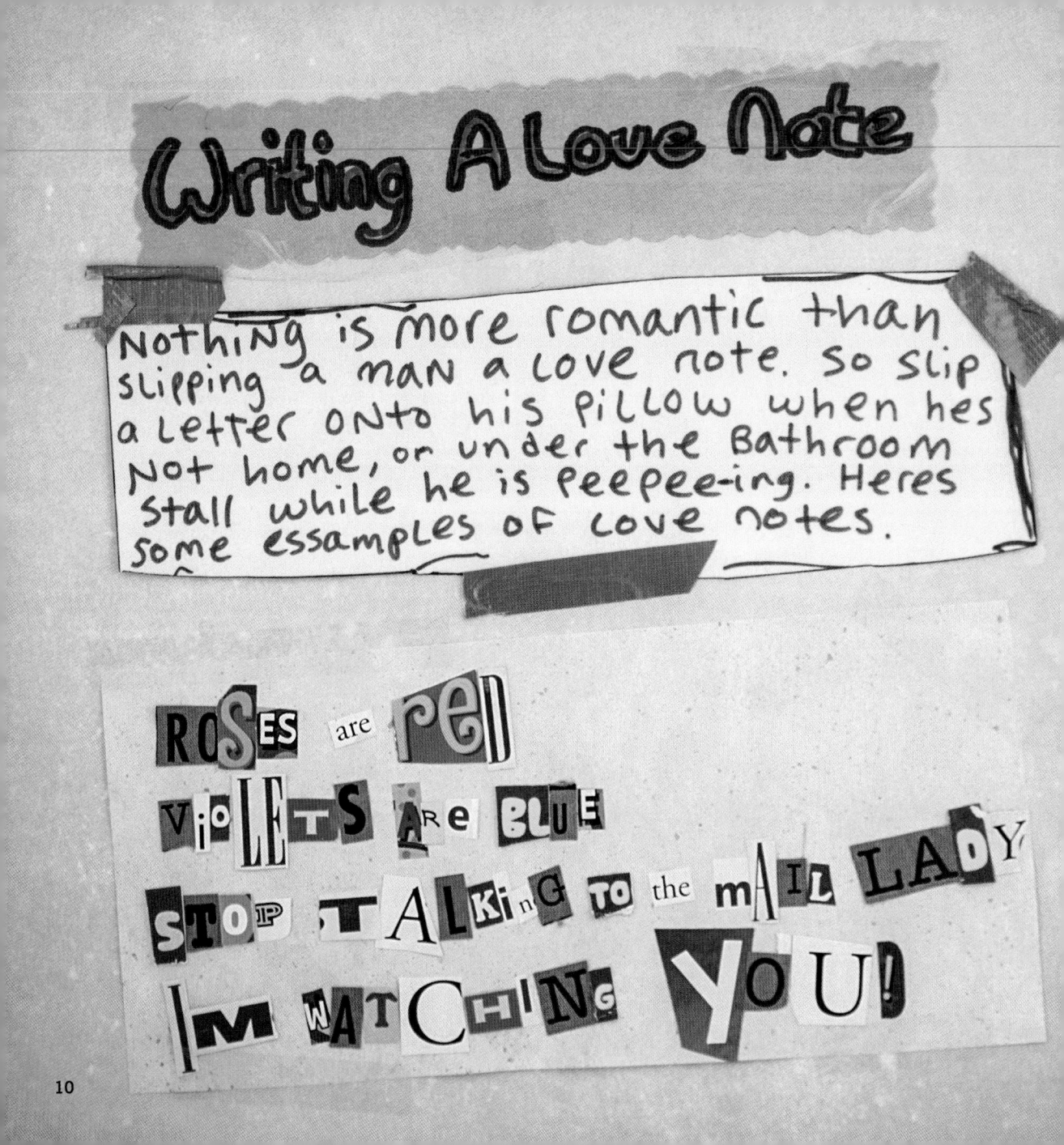
Writing A Love Note
Nothing is more romantic than slipping a man a love note. So slip a letter onto his pillow when hes Not home, or under the Bathroom stall while he is peepee-ing. Heres some essamples of love notes.
ROSES are red
VIOLETS Are BLUE
STOP TALKING TO the MAIL LADY
IM WATCHING YOU!

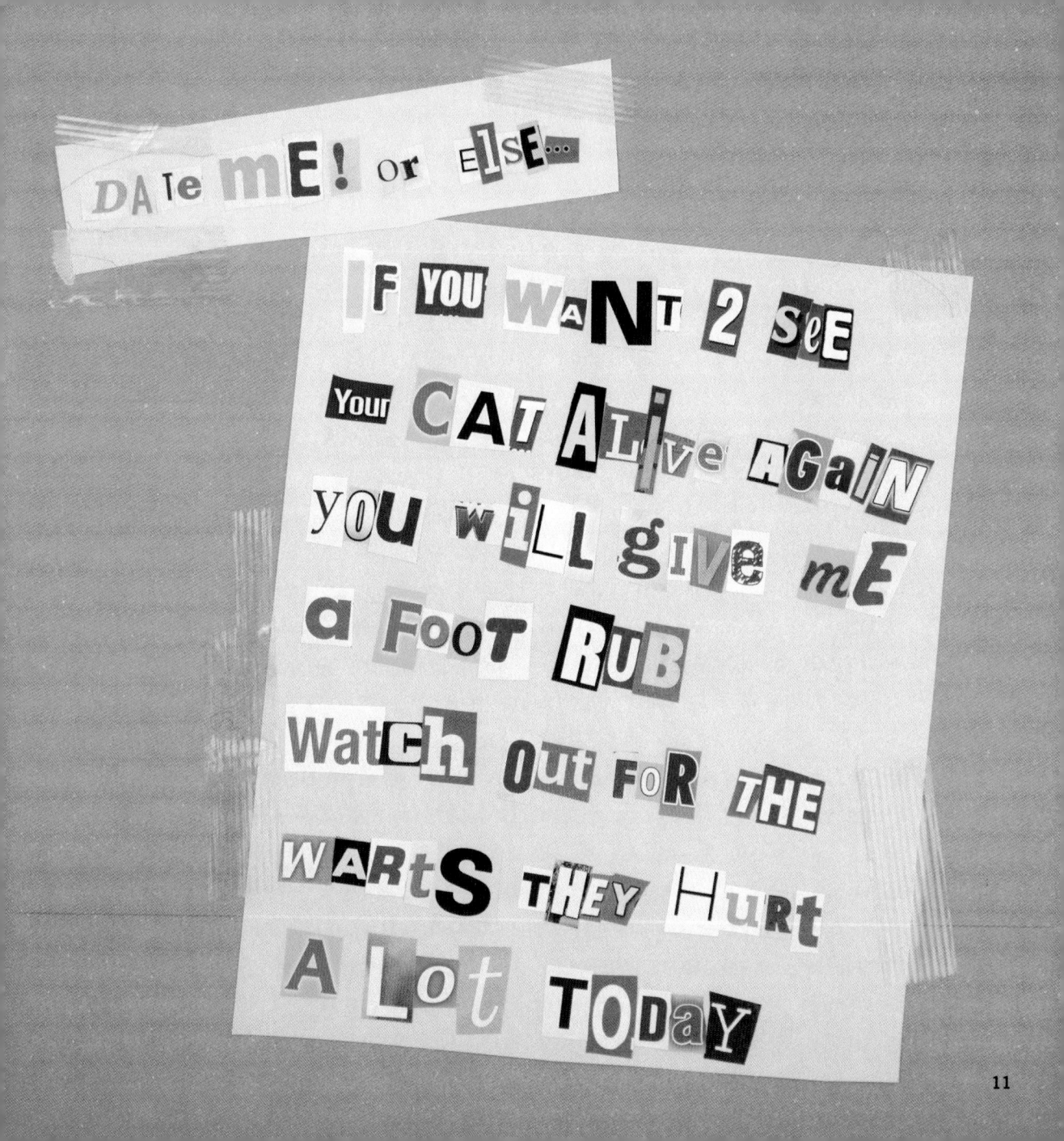
DAte mE! or ElSE...
IF YOU WANT 2 SEE
YOUR CAT ALIVE AGAIN
YOU WILL GIVE mE
a FOOT RUB
Watch OUT FOR THE
WARtS THEY Hurt
A Lot TODAY

Levels of a relationship
Level 1 stranger.
Level 2 mine.
Level 3 Bae
Level 4 Husband
Level 5 servant
Level 6 Prisoner
Level 7 widow

My uncle wrote out the difrent bases in touching in relatchonships
BEFORE YOU START RUNNING THE BASES, YOU NEED TO BE SURE YOU'RE READY TO PLAY THE GAME IN THE FIRST PLACE. I'M TALKING TRAINING, PRACTICE, A LITTLE T-BALL IF YOU KNOW WHAT I MEAN.
1ST
HOME RUN
FIRST BASE
FIRST CONTACT/FIRST LOOK. LOVE A FIRST SIGHT? YES. FIRST BASE IS STARING. COULD BE ACROSS THE ROOM, THROUGH A WINDOW. LOTS OF OPTIONS.
HOME RUN
THIS IS YOUR FIRST KISS. IT'S LIKE EATING THE LAST PLUMB OF THE SEASON. YOUR LIPS GUSH WITH JUICE AS IT RUNS DOWN ITS SKIN AND YOUR TONGUE RUNS ACROSS THE TENDER FLESH BURSTING WITH FLAVOR. IT'S LIKE THAT.
SECOND BASE
BASE TWO: THE MASSAGE. A GENTLE RUB ON THE NECK, BACK OR SHOULDER CAN EXPRESS YOUR FEELINGS. THIS IS A GREAT WAY TO CONNECT WITH SOMEONE, I USE IT ON MY CUSTOMERS ALL THE TIME.
THIRD BASE
THIS BASE IS CUDDLING. UNLESS YOU'RE FAMILY YOU SHOULD WAIT TO CUDDLE UNTIL YOU GET MARRIED.
3RD
2ND
BASES IN A RELATIONSHIP

First Date

Movies

The nice thing about movies is its quiet so its a grate place to Talk and get to know each other.

Uncles House

very private place where you can play with your Daddy saddle.

Conversation Topics

- yourself
- How many kids do you want?
- How much money do you have?
- what diseases run in yor family?
- Types of Yarn
- Do you mind genital warts

First Date Eddikate

3 ways to play hard to get.

its good to act uninterested in your first date to leave him wanting more.

1. PHYSICALLY — punch them, hit them, spit near them, pull a hair.

2. VERBALLY — tell them they are ugly

3. EMOTIONALLY — act ~~un-inter~~ uninterested and bored to hurt their feelings

marriage

Now that you've been on a date, your ready for marriage.

marriage is about 3 things

1. A dress.
2. a cake.
3. making other people jealous.

Wedding Vows

its important 2 write your own vows Because traditional vows have promises you wont Be able to Keep. I wrote some 4 you to use.

i, miranda take you, Bae...to Be my husband.
I promise to Be the Best person in this relatchonship.
For Im Better your worse
im richer, your poorer
your sick im in health
as Long as you Shall Live.
Amen.

Changing the person you Love.

People often say that you cant change a person. That is Not true. People who say that are just Lazy. Hear are some ways you can change someone

NOT ThoughtFuL?

Talk to them in their sleep to influence there thoughts

Never Buys you gifts?

Buy things for yourself with his credit card

Disagrees with you?
Yell at him untill he does
Not a good dresser?
Burn all his clothes and get him new ones
Looks at other woman?
Put a blanket over her head
Doesnt express his feelings?
See next page

Expressing your feelings is HARD.

iF you or someone you No has ProBLems expressing itself just Look at this List of feelings and check Boxes that match you Best.

- ☐ SAD
- ☐ happy
- ☐ excited
- ☐ angry
- ☐ depressed
- ☐ Bored
- ☐ hungry
- ☐ awake
- ☐ OK
- ☐ asLeep
- ☐ wet
- ☐ tired
- ☐ sticky
- ☐ singy
- ☐ cry-y
- ☐ FULL
- ☐ Loud
- ☐ other

how to cuddle

Back to Back

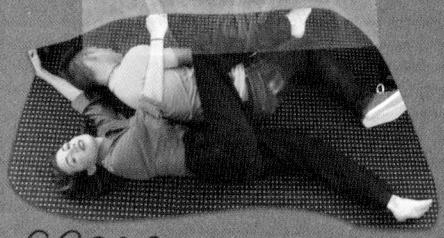

spoon

in the womb

cuddeling is important in a marriage because it s when you touch for the first time. hear are the cuddeling positchons.

Christian

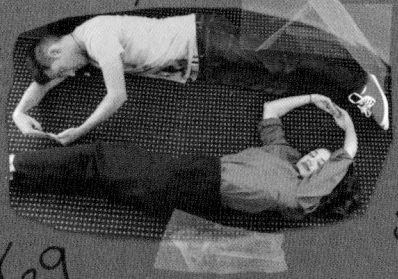

69

Sharing air

the uncle

Breaking up.

YouTube Video: Great way to get more views

Twitter: use hashtags like #BreakingUp or #OnTheProwl

Text Message

Invite them on a date with your NEW boyfriend.

Ring Box

HEARTACHE

sometimes the boy will brake up with you. if this happens you will need to learn how to get over a broken heart because no one likes being around sad people. its anoying. How you get over a broken heart is to stop being sad. Easy. or get revenge. (see next page 4 details.

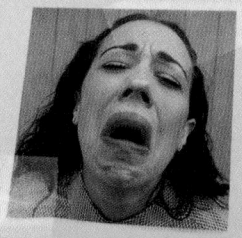

Getting Revenge

- ☐ spit in his drink
- ☐ kick a bush in his yard
- ☐ catch a fly and let it go in his bedroom (make sure its a loud one)
- ☐ Put hair in his mouth
- ☐ crunch up all his cereal and put it back in the box
- ☐ Dont talk to him
- ☐ Kiss something in front of him
- ☐ cut the erasers off his pencils

LOVE QUIZ

WHAT KIND OF BAE ARE YOU?

(results on next page)

where would you go on a date?

a. uncles house - 3 points
b. beach - 1 point
c. nothing - 2 point

how do you kiss?

a. on mouth - 1 point
b. on hand - 3 points
c. hairs - 2 points

what's your type?

a. bad boy - 1 point
b. model - 2 points
c. that guy at the park - 3 points

what kind of pet do u want?

a. dog - 2 points
b. snake - 1 points
c. ant farm - 3 points

what do you like for dinner?

a. spagehtti - 1 point
b. celery - 2 points
c. salami - 3 points

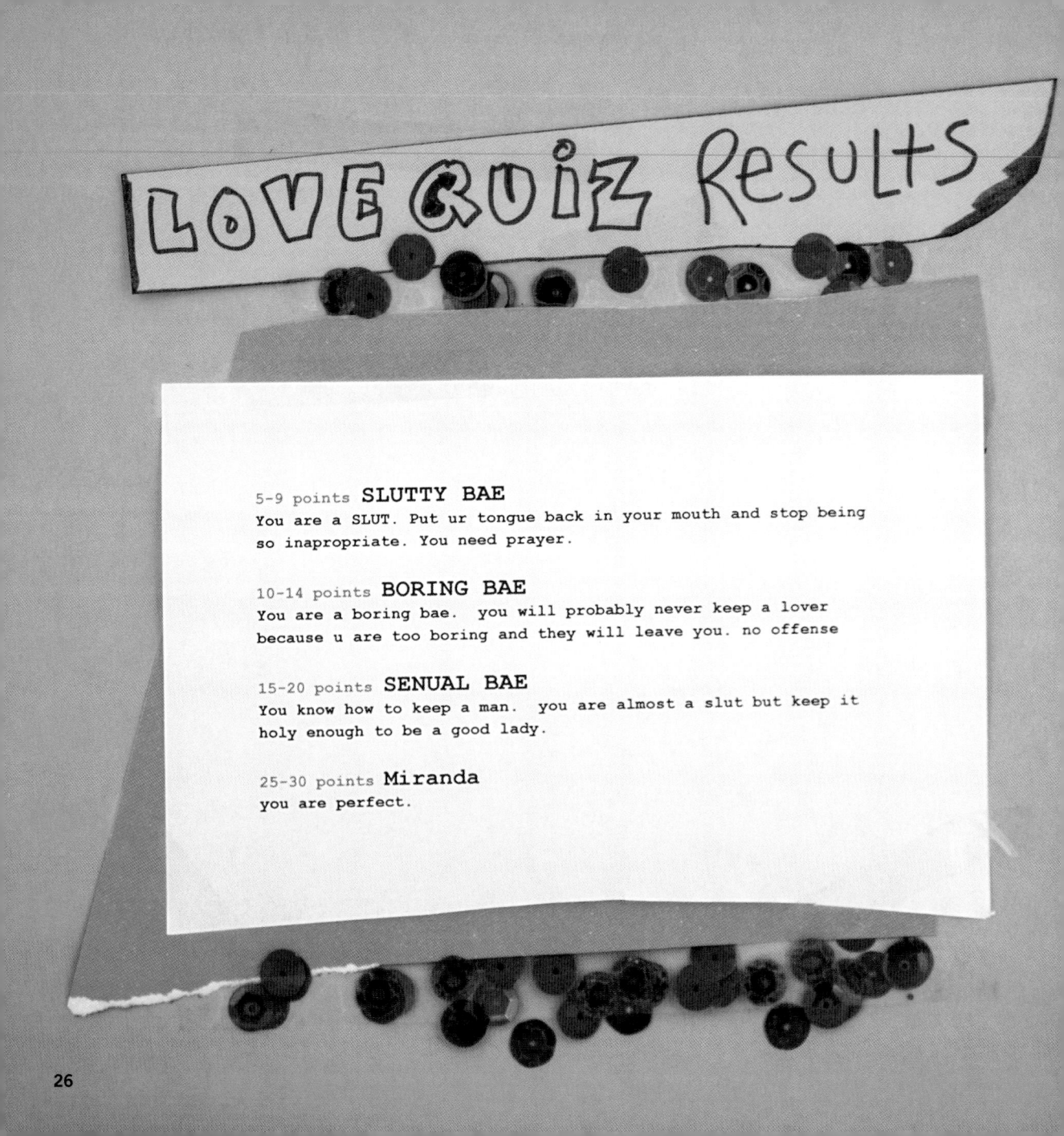

LOVE QUIZ Results

5-9 points **SLUTTY BAE**
You are a SLUT. Put ur tongue back in your mouth and stop being so inapropriate. You need prayer.

10-14 points **BORING BAE**
You are a boring bae. you will probably never keep a lover because u are too boring and they will leave you. no offense

15-20 points **SENUAL BAE**
You know how to keep a man. you are almost a slut but keep it holy enough to be a good lady.

25-30 points **Miranda**
you are perfect.

TALENT

In this chapter i will
Tech you how to
Have a talent
cuz you probly
dont have one.

Which Talents do you Have?

Check the Talents you Have

- ☐ singing
- ☐ acting
- ☐ Dancing
- ☐ model
- ☐ magichen
- ☐ drawing
- ☐ dressing up cats
- ☐ eating
- ☐ gardening
- ☐ PHoto making
- ☐ cooking
- ☐ jumping
- ☐ Loom bracelets
- ☐ sleeping
- ☐ cursive
- ☐ swimming
- ☐ whistling

Some people have 3 or 4 of these. I have them all so in case you dont have a talents i will tech you some.

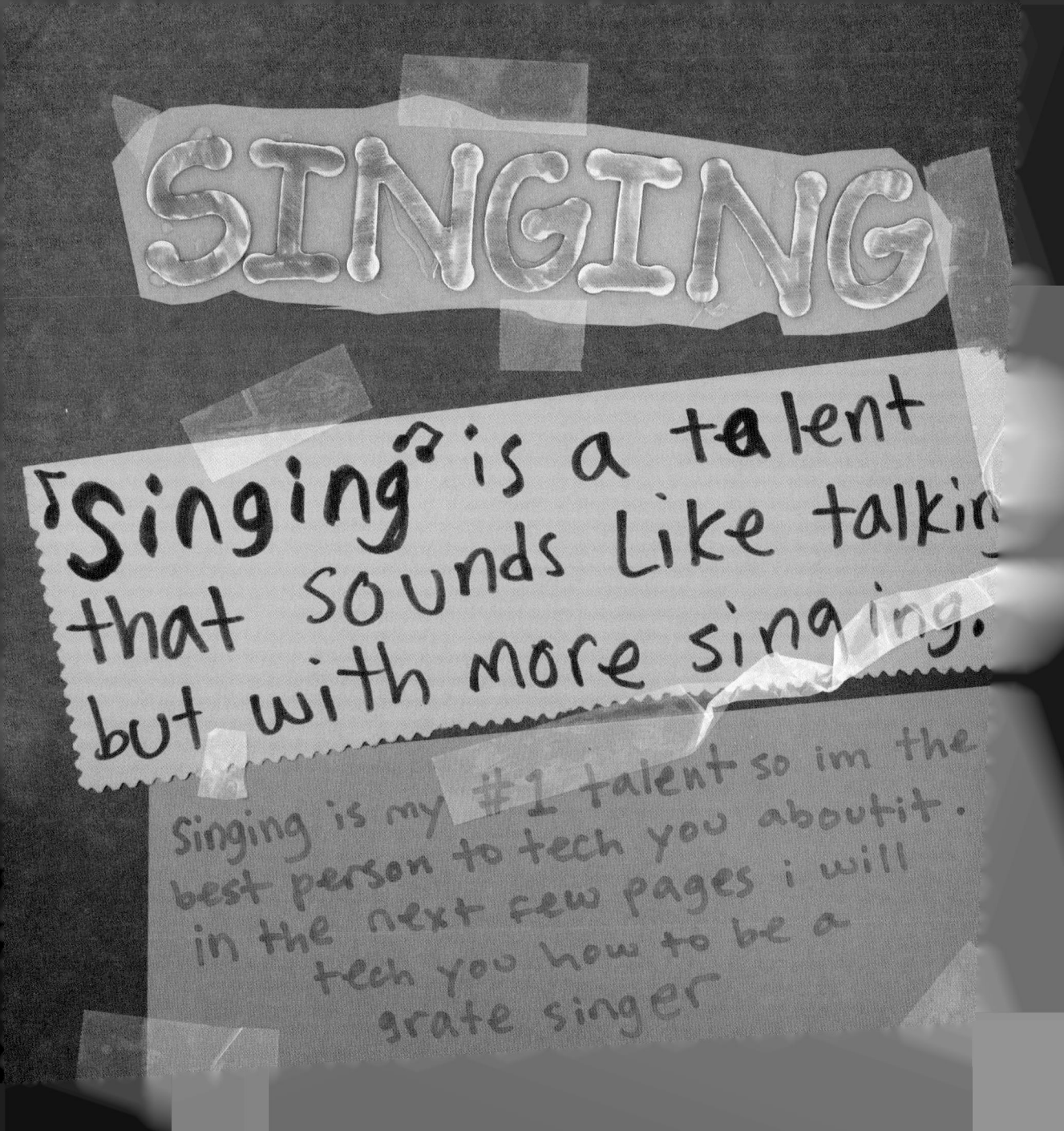
SINGING
Singing is a talent that sounds Like talkin but with more singing.
Singing is my #1 talent so im the best person to tech you aboutit. in the next few pages i will tech you how to be a grate singer

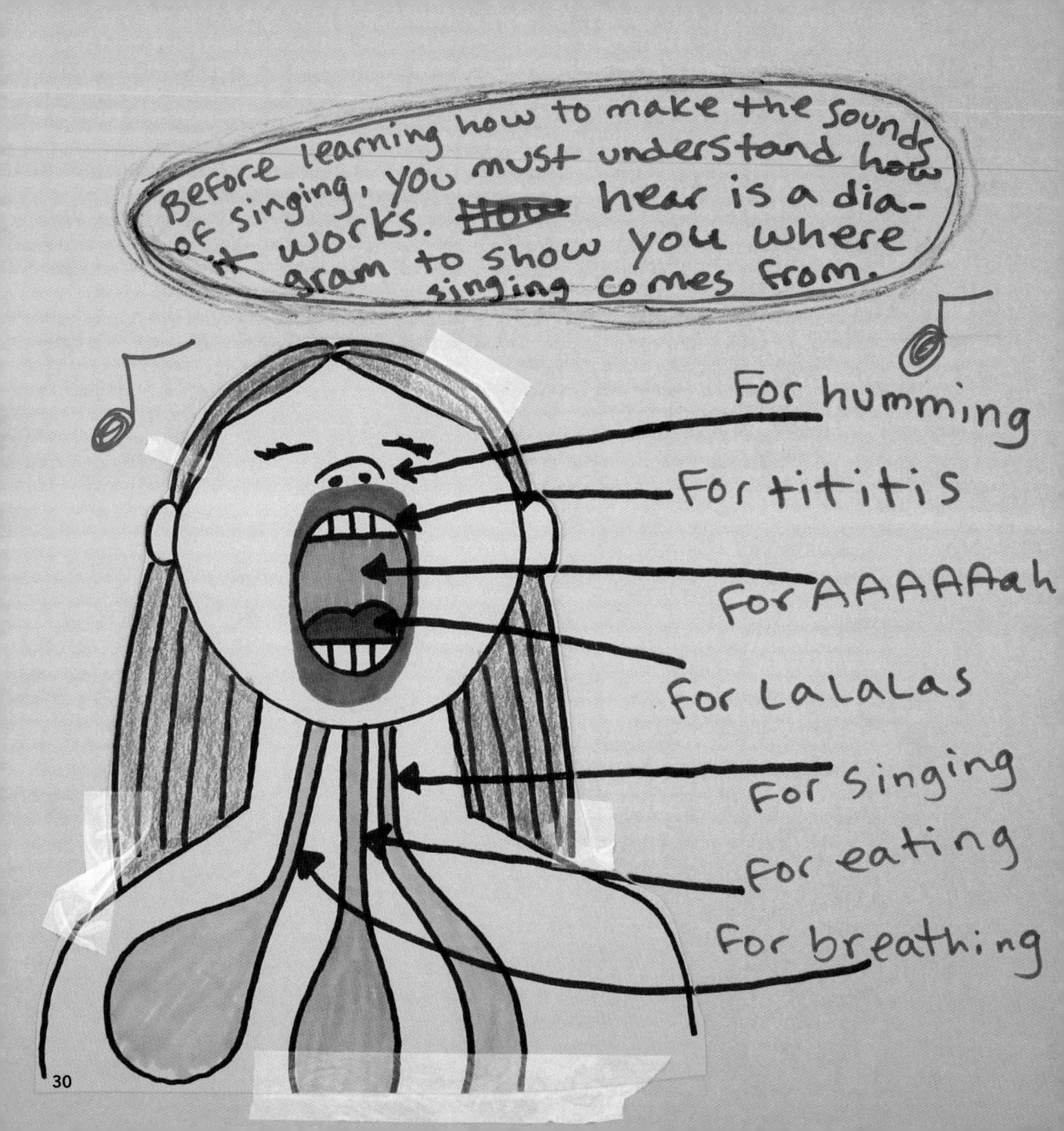
Before learning how to make the sounds of singing, you must understand how it works. ~~How~~ hear is a diagram to show you where singing comes from.
For humming
For tititis
For AAAAAAah
For LaLaLas
For singing
For eating
For breathing

Vibrato

vibrato is that shaking sound your voice makes. Shake a part of your body and it shakes your voice. I shake my head.

The BIGGER the shake, the bigger the Vibrato

Learning Music
Learning music is important because you need to learn how to learn music. some People will give you music that looks like this
That makes no sense so just use a piano.
Lowest note you can sing
Chopsticks
high note i can hit but you probly cant
*if you dont have a piano just pretend.

DANCING
DANCING IS A GREAT TALENT TO HAVE BECAUSE YOU CAN DO IT TO MUSIC OR NOT. HEAR ARE SOME GOOD DANCE MOVES
MOON WALK
SINGLE LADY
THE WORM
TWERKING
scan to wach how to twerk appropriatly

IN order to dance goodly
you need good tEchneek.
Ballet is the Best way
to getit

BALLet Positchons

repeat.

DANCING
HIP HOP
Hands out
Ballet
Hands up
ROBOT
Karate hands
TAP
Jazz hands

NOW YOU KNOW HOW TO DANCE BUT

BEWARE

dancing can be dangerous. Some dancing is very inna-propriate and can make others Lust.

Dance moves to stay away from

Michael Jackson

The Twerk

The prom

Pole dance

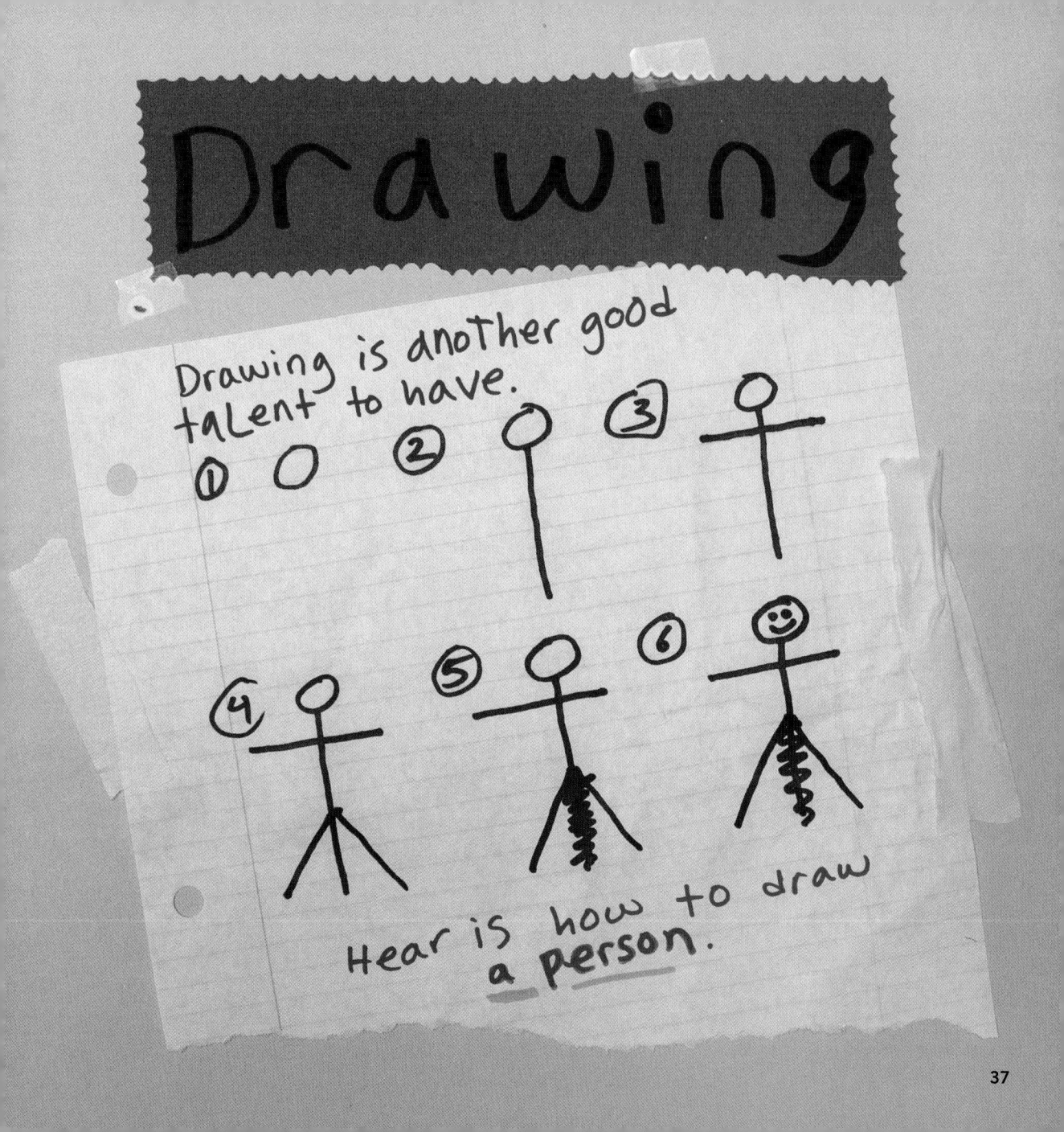
Drawing
Drawing is another good talent to have.
1
2
3
4
5
6
Hear is how to draw a person.

How to draw a Hot DOG
1
Draw weiner
2
Fill it in
3
add the Bun
4
Add relish
5
Add ketchup
6
DO NOT EAT

ACTING

For This Talent you have to be good with your face. Try these etspressions.

happy

sad

confused

healthy

disappointed

smart

Pritty

titked off

Tired

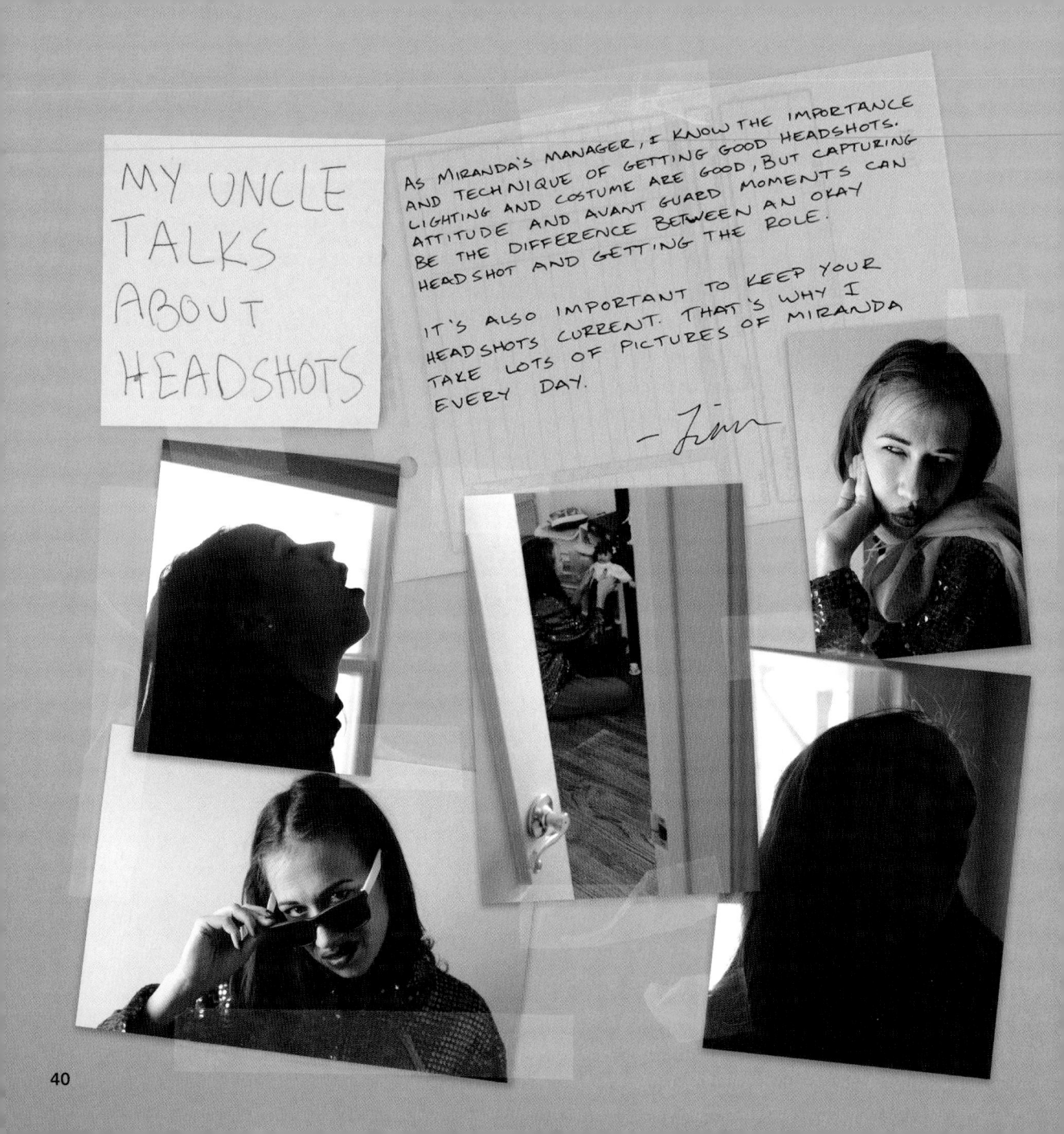
MY UNCLE TALKS ABOUT HEADSHOTS
AS MIRANDA'S MANAGER, I KNOW THE IMPORTANCE AND TECHNIQUE OF GETTING GOOD HEADSHOTS. LIGHTING AND COSTUME ARE GOOD, BUT CAPTURING ATTITUDE AND AVANT GUARD MOMENTS CAN BE THE DIFFERENCE BETWEEN AN OKAY HEADSHOT AND GETTING THE ROLE.
IT'S ALSO IMPORTANT TO KEEP YOUR HEADSHOTS CURRENT. THAT'S WHY I TAKE LOTS OF PICTURES OF MIRANDA EVERY DAY.
- Jim

MAGIC

MAGIC works By Lying.

step one: Lie
its not going to disapear.

Step two - Lie
Theres nothing over there

step three - Lie.
it did not disapear.

step 4 - Lie.
it is under my shirt.

Dressing Up CATS

This is a gr8 skill because it makes cats better and more like people.

Talent Awards

Cut out the award that you earned.

Singing

Draws Good

acting

Majic

Other

Good effort/No talent

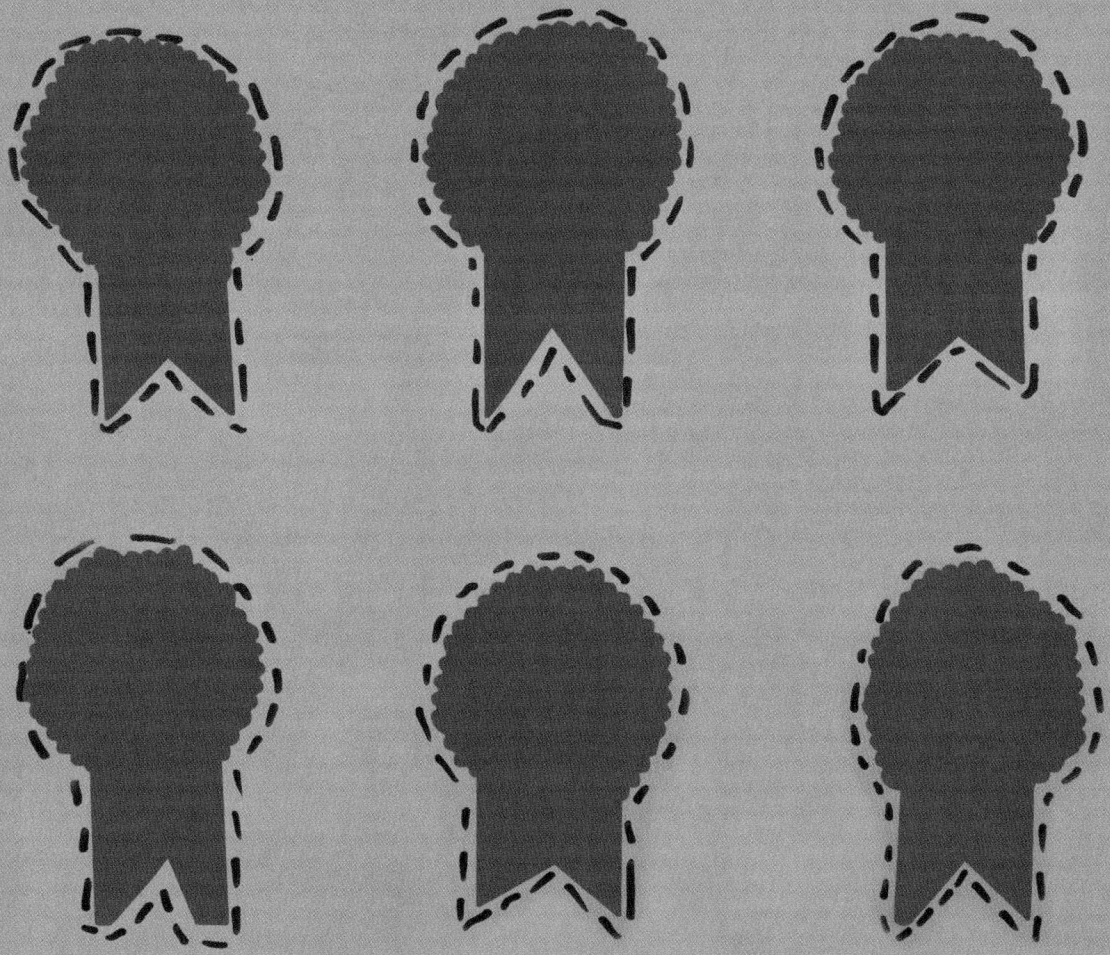

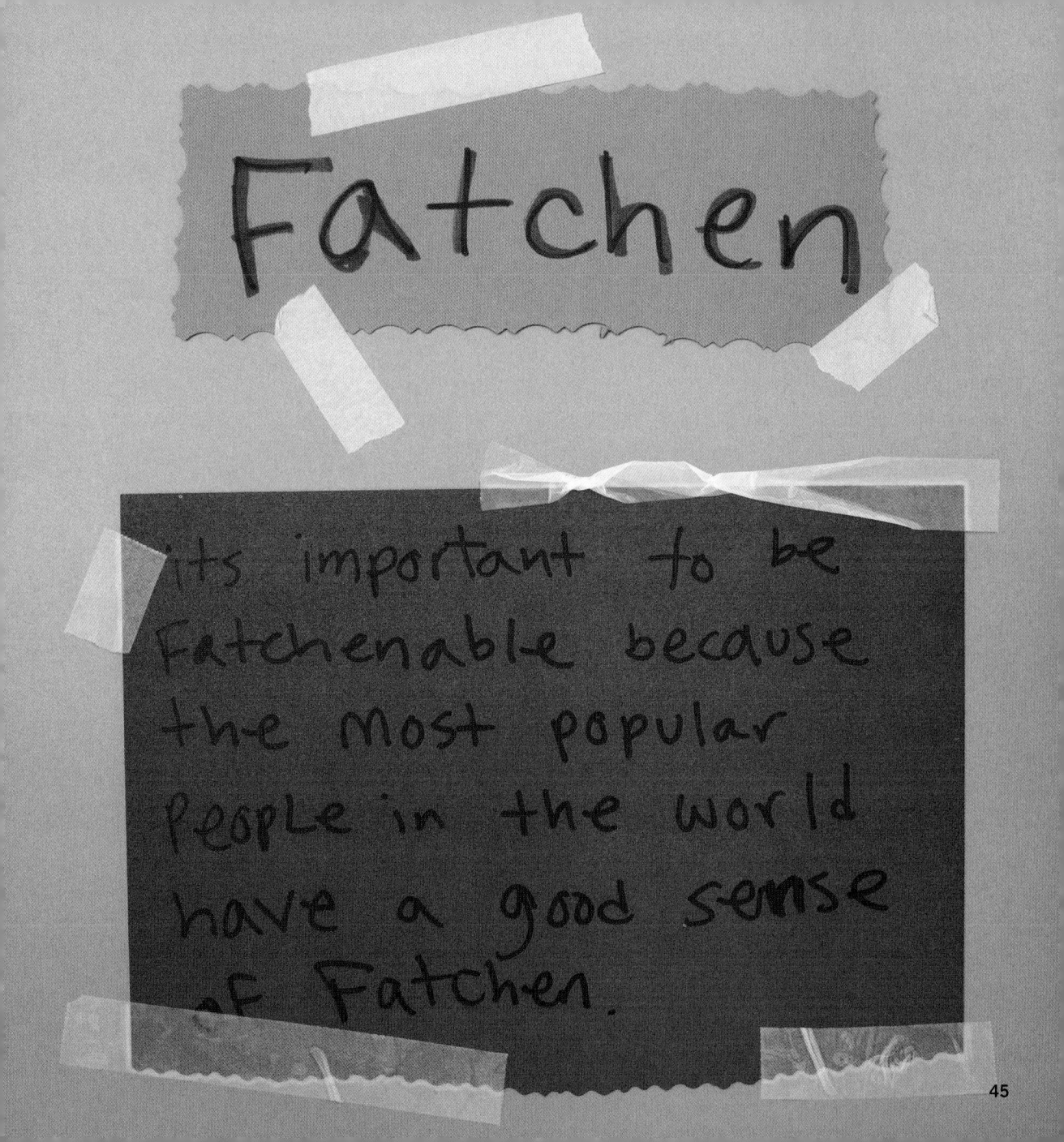
Fatchen
its important to be
Fatchenable because
the most popular
people in the world
have a good sense
of Fatchen.

Clothes say a Lot about a person. For example: "I am not naked." or "I am wearing clothes."

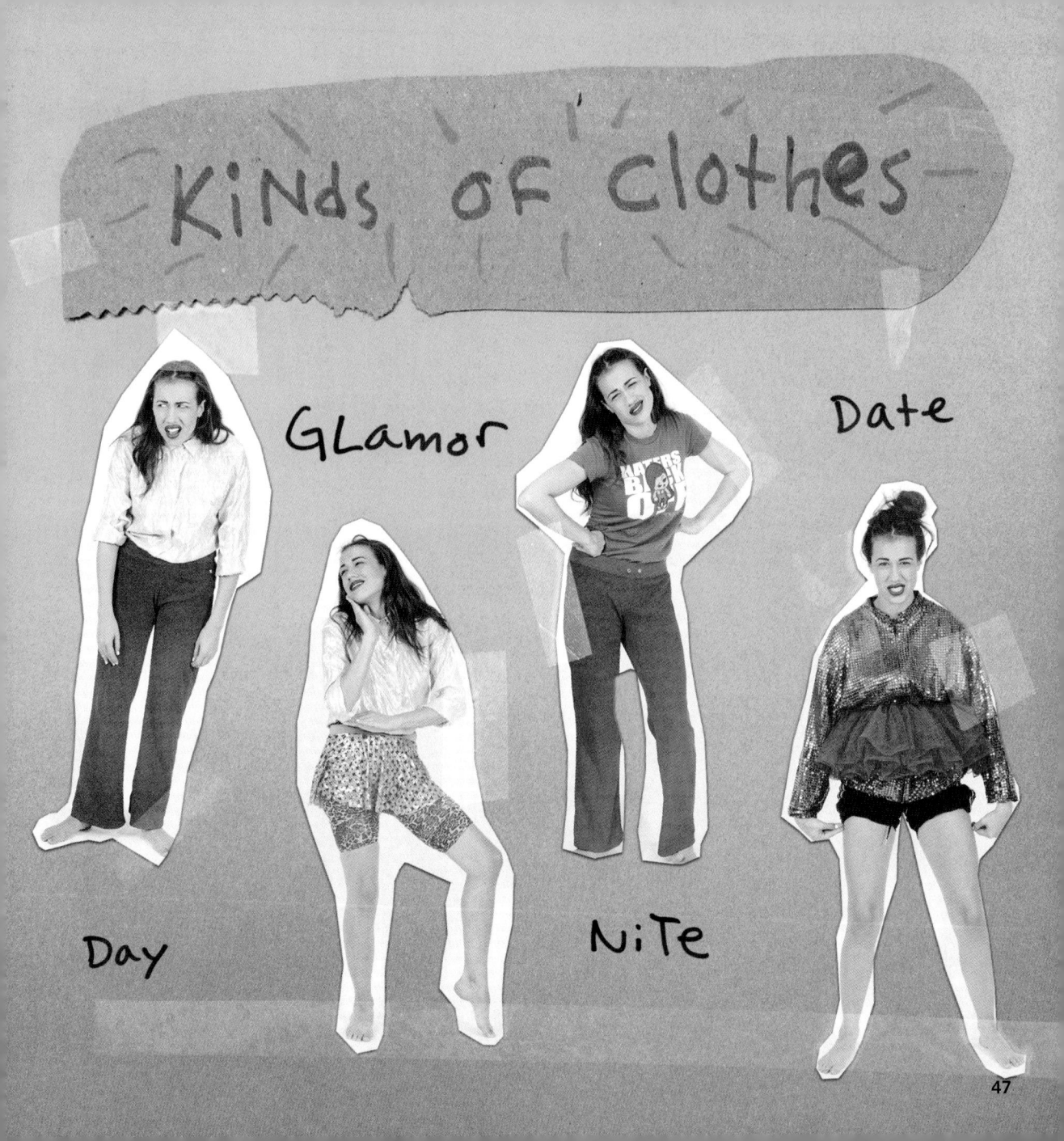
Kinds of clothes
Glamor
Date
Day
Nite

Shoes are the window to the soul.
Business
Fun
Slut
Hungry
other.
Know what your shoes mean.

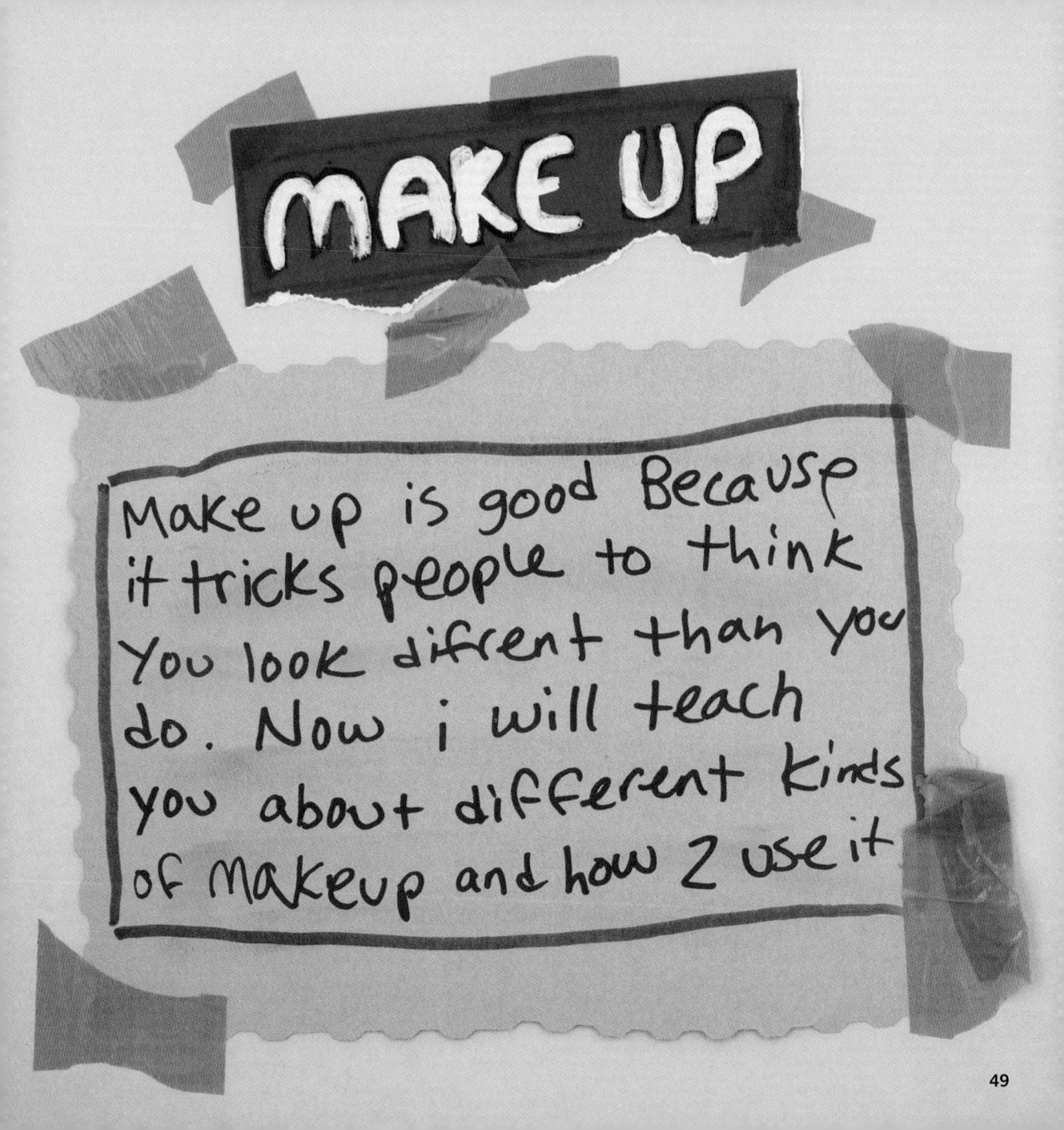

MAKE UP

Make up is good Becausp
it tricks people to think
You look difrent than you
do. Now i will teach
you about different kinds
of makeup and how 2 use it

EYE BROWS

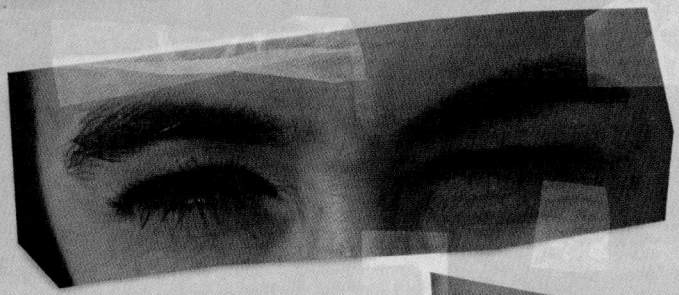

NATURAL

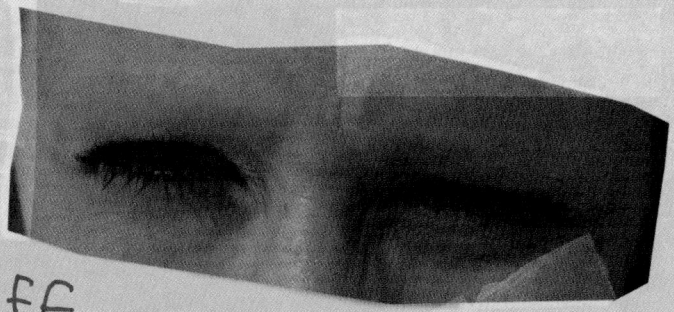

Shave them off

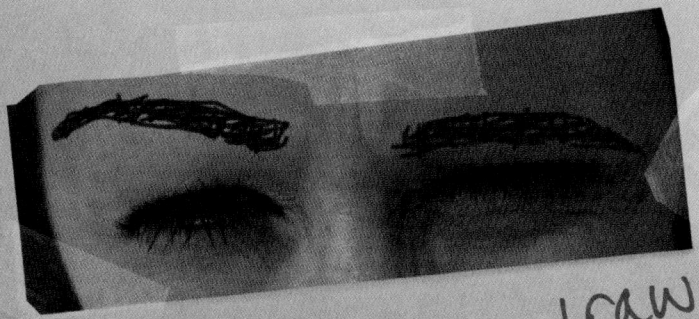

draw them on.

Always ware lots of
Listick to essentuate
your Lips
Listick
Put it
here

Eye Make Up

Eyeshadews R fun cuz its like facepaint kind of. hear are some looks for you2 try.

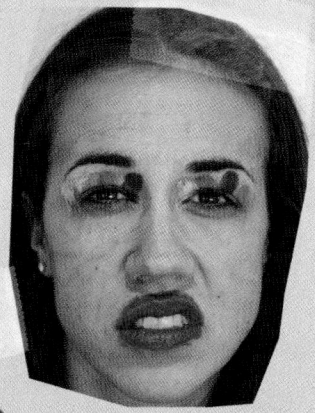

Rainbow

Cat eye

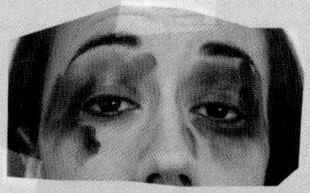

smokey

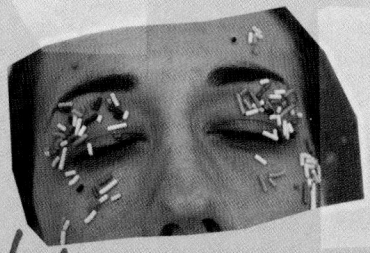

Sprinkles

if you dont have eyeshadows at home you can make make up out of these things.
crayon
paint
candy
blueberry
this
puffy cheese snack

OTHER EYE MAKE-UPS

EYE-LINER

eye liner is pokey and dangerous.
i do not recomend.

MASCARA

mascara is pokey and dangerous.
i do not recomend

FAKE EYELATCHES

Fake eyelatches are pokey and dangerous 4 your eyes.
hear are other ways you can use them.

mustash

Finger wigs

FACE MAKE UPS
FOUNDATCHON
This is like face paint. Girls use a lot of it to hide zits and to look oranger.
put it hear
BLUNCH
put this on your cheeks to look more girl. lipstick doubles as blunch
Put it hear
BRONZER
This makes you look like another race. This is illegal. dont use it.
Dont put it anywear

HAIRS
DONT over Brush
Keep hairs out of Face wit Hair Pins
Also hai
Keep Leftover hairs for crafts and DOLL projects
these

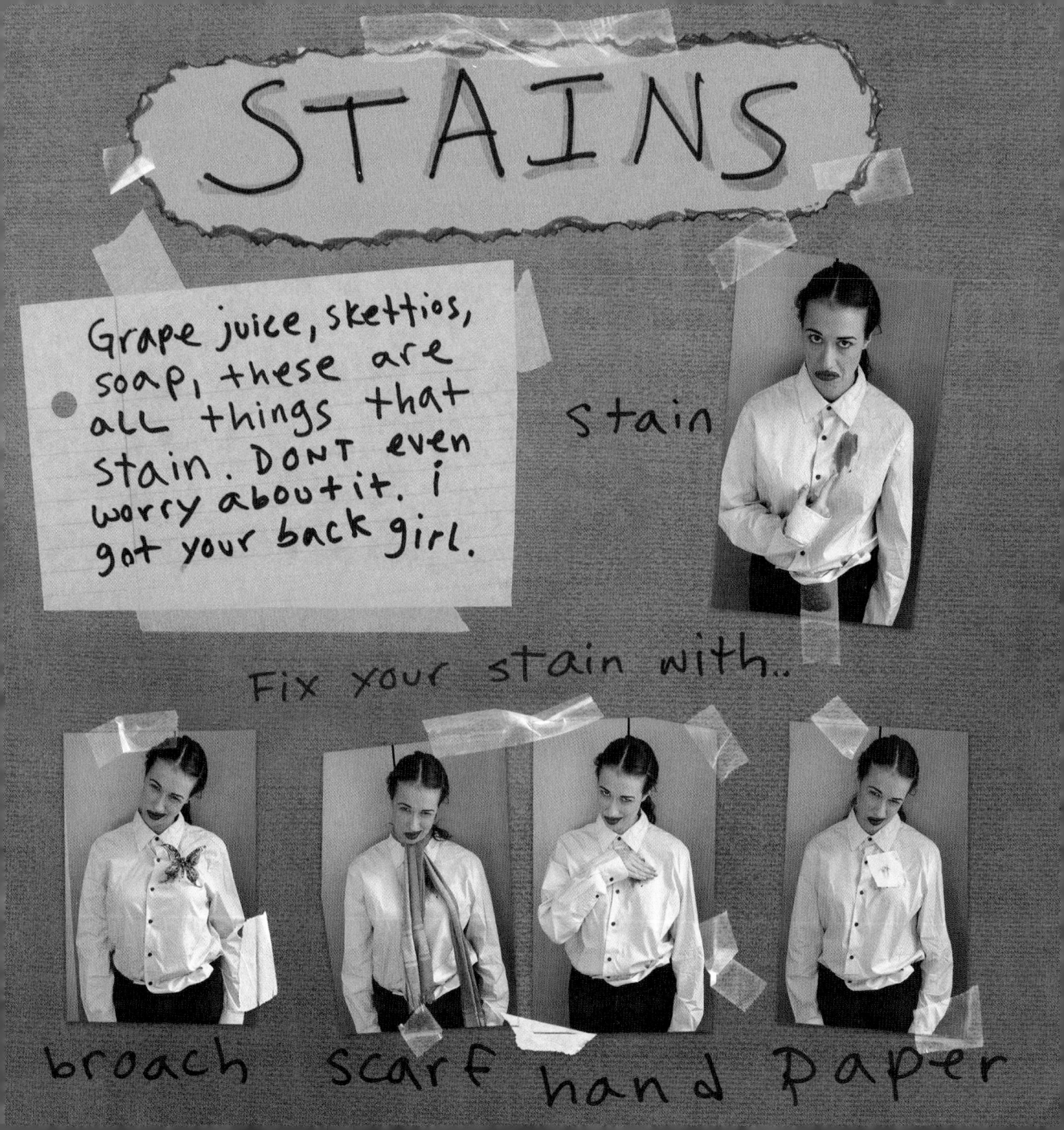
STAINS
Grape juice, skettios, soap, these are all things that stain. DONT even worry about it. i got your back girl.
stain
Fix your stain with..
broach
scarf
hand
paper

Accessories

you put these on your clothes and skin to look more fancier hear are my favorit accessorries.

HaTS

Necklace

braslet

socks

bag

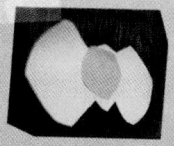
bows

rings

scarf

stickers

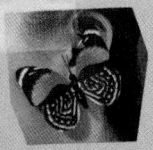
earrings

purses

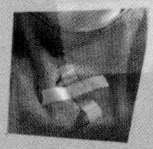
tape

balloons

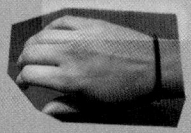
hairties

String

animals

swords

box

headbands

Make your own jewelry

Jewelry is expensive so hear i will show you how you can make your own.

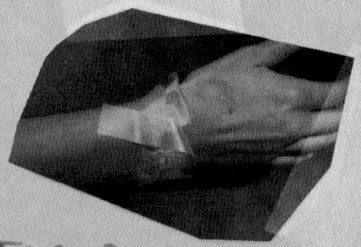

Tape Bracelet

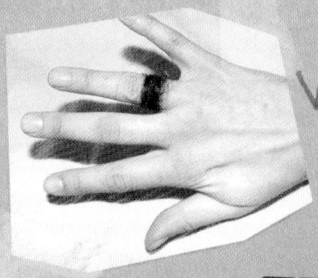

hair Ring

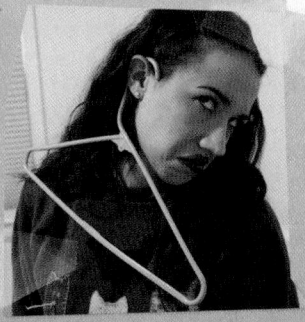

hanger earrings

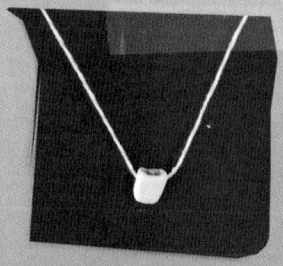

tooth neklace

PORN

There are lots of diffrent kinds of porn. The pitcher below shows a few esamples.

How Not To Be Porn!
Button to the top
Loos shirt
pull up pants
cover to your ankles
DO NOT BE PORN

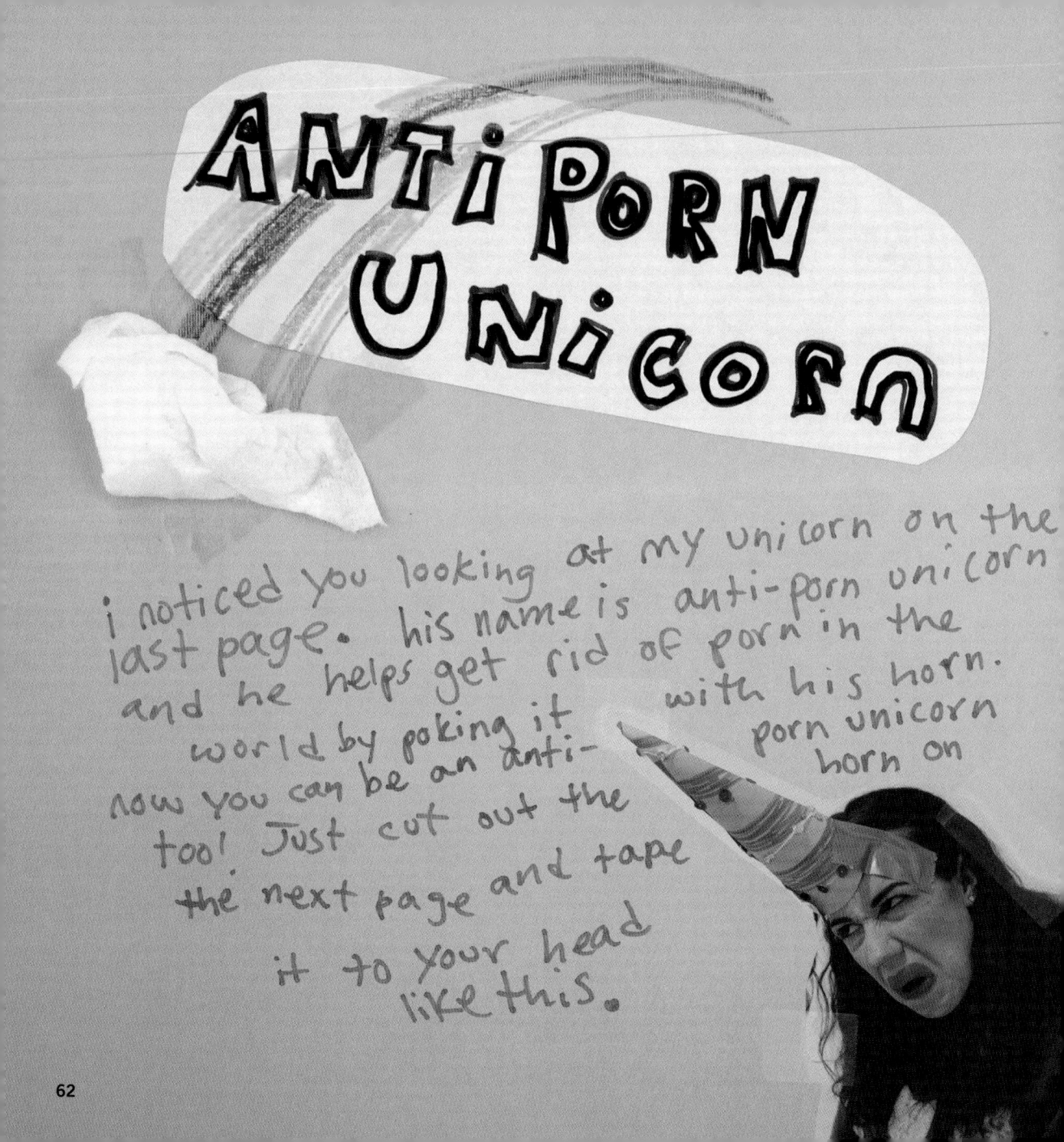
AntiPorn Unicorn
i noticed you looking at my unicorn on the last page. his name is anti-porn unicorn and he helps get rid of porn in the world by poking it with his horn. now you can be an anti-porn unicorn too! Just cut out the horn on the next page and tape it to your head like this.

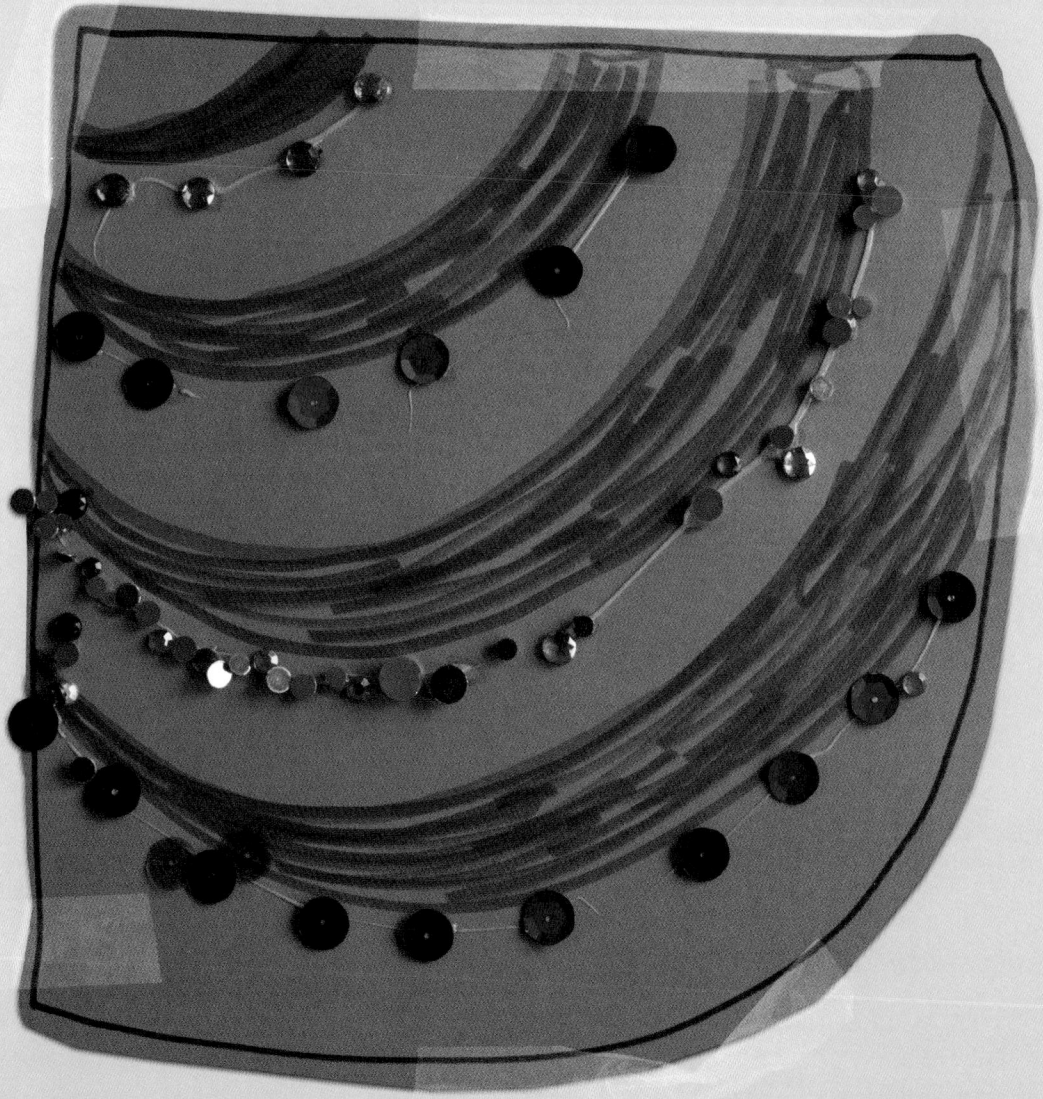

MODELING

Now that you look fachonable, you need to learn how to act fachonable. This is called being a model. i will teach you how to look like a model. if you are ugly turn the page.

MODEL POSES

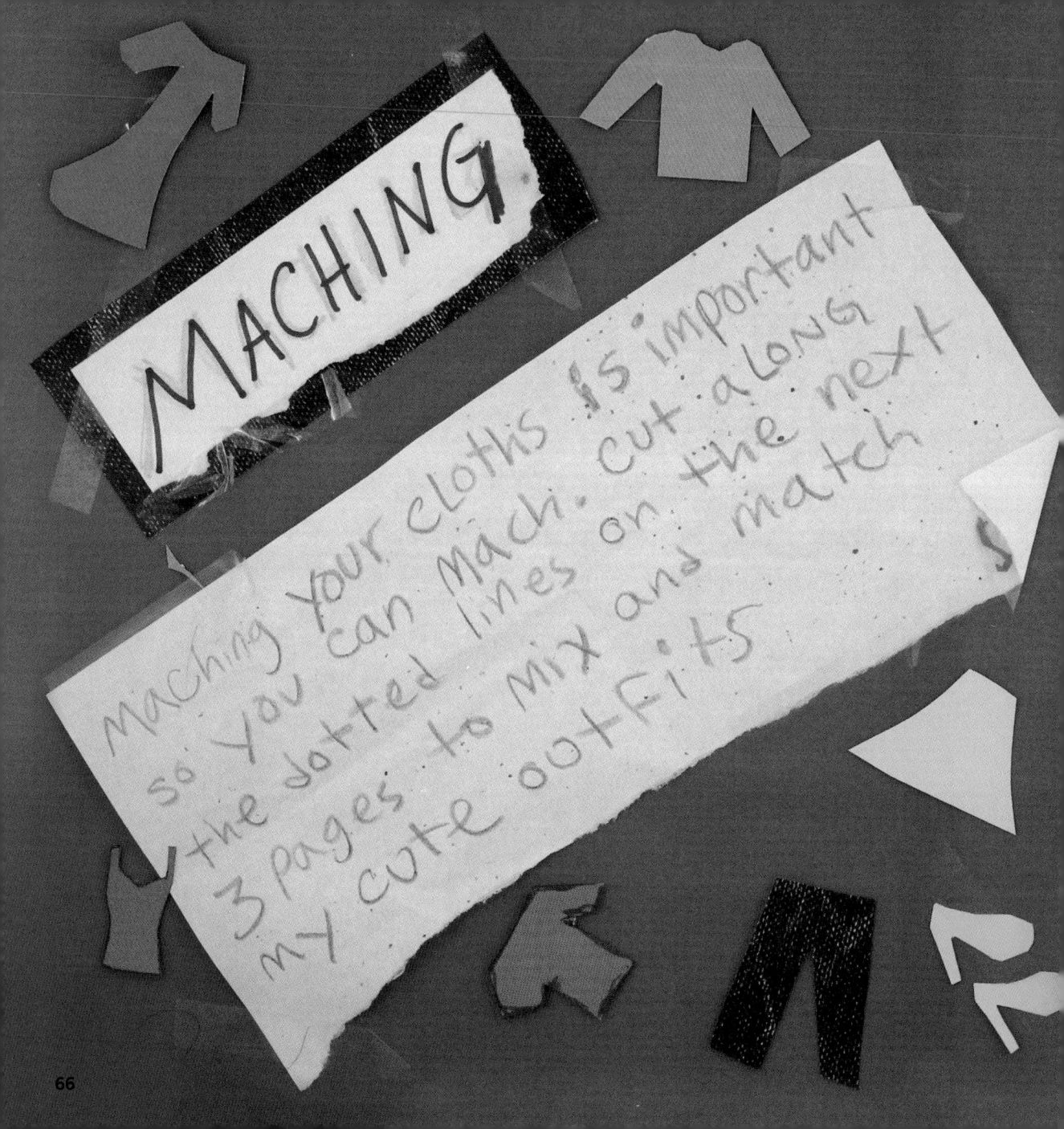
MACHING
Maching your cloths is important
so you can mach. cut along
the dotted lines on the next
3 pages to mix and match
my cute outfits

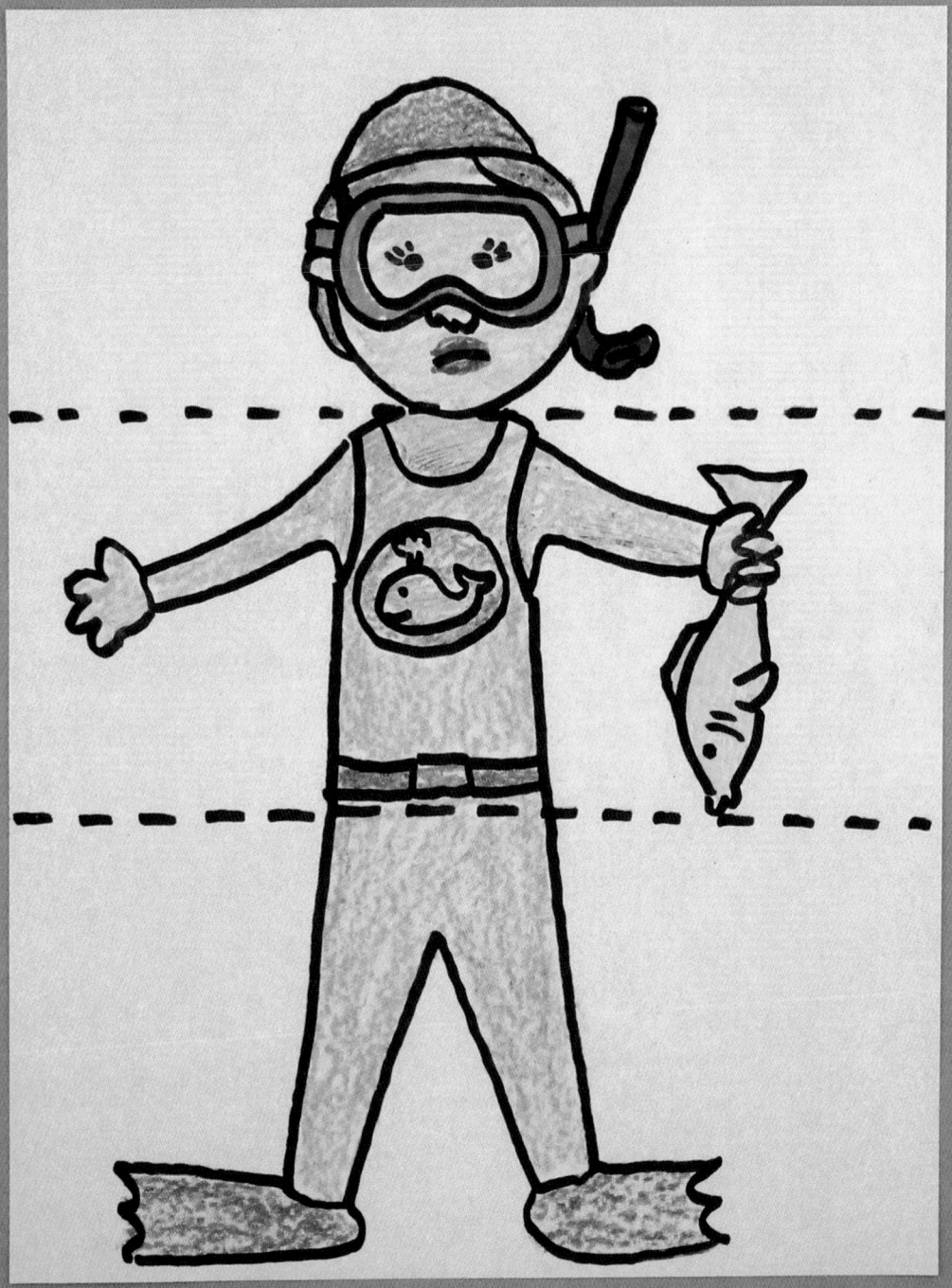

CAREER

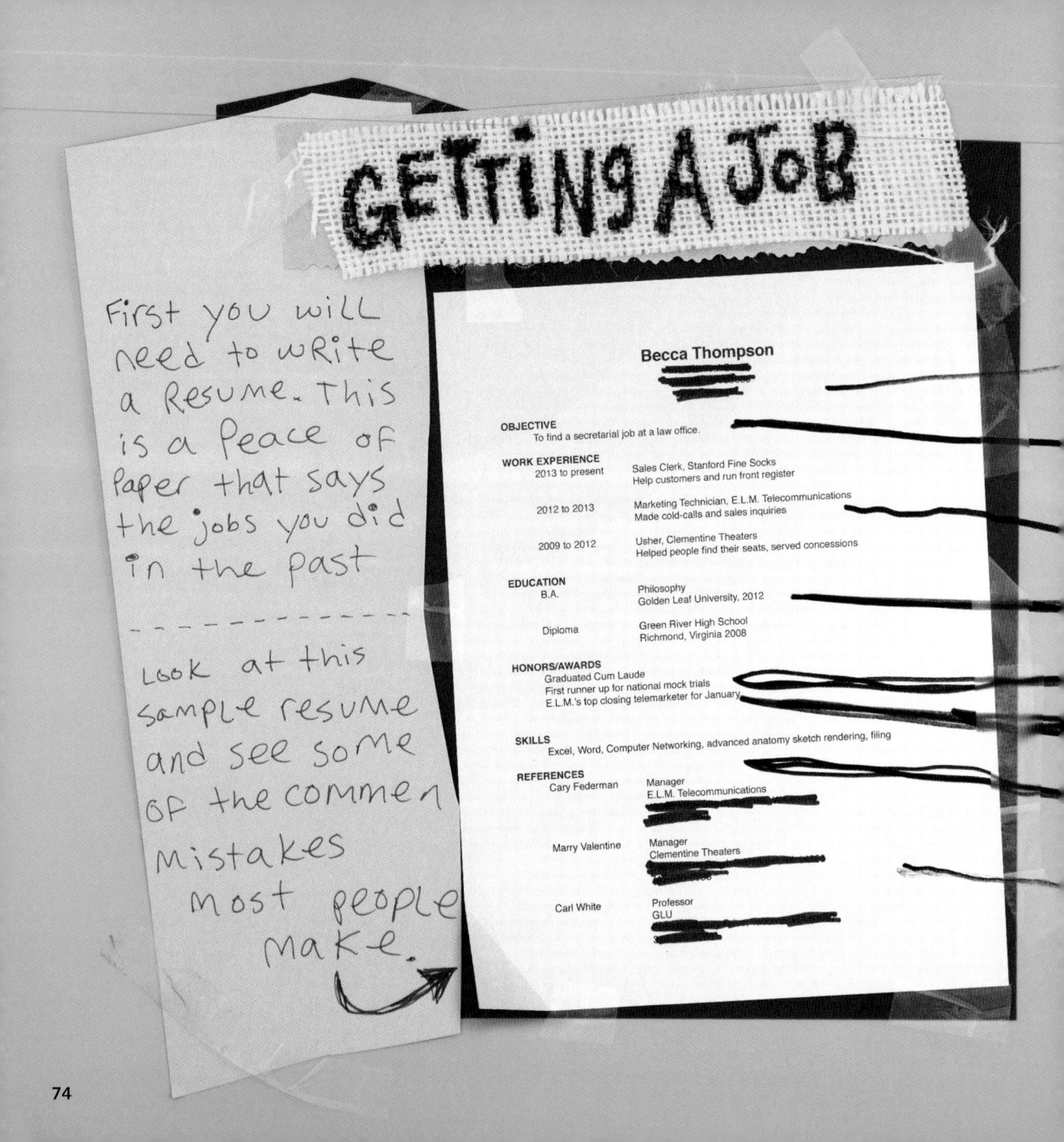
GETTING A JOB
First you will need to write a Resume. This is a Peace of Paper that says the jobs you did in the past
Look at this sample resume and see some of the commen mistakes most people make.
Becca Thompson
OBJECTIVE
To find a secretarial job at a law office.
WORK EXPERIENCE
2013 to present
Sales Clerk, Stanford Fine Socks
Help customers and run front register
2012 to 2013
Marketing Technician, E.L.M. Telecommunications
Made cold-calls and sales inquiries
2009 to 2012
Usher, Clementine Theaters
Helped people find their seats, served concessions
EDUCATION
B.A.
Philosophy
Golden Leaf University, 2012
Diploma
Green River High School
Richmond, Virginia 2008
HONORS/AWARDS
Graduated Cum Laude
First runner up for national mock trials
E.L.M.'s top closing telemarketer for January
SKILLS
Excel, Word, Computer Networking, advanced anatomy sketch rendering, filing
REFERENCES
Cary Federman
Manager
E.L.M. Telecommunications
Marry Valentine
Manager
Clementine Theaters
Carl White
Professor
GLU

Problems With Resume

Too much Blank Space you should Pack it up with more Bragging.

This is a Boring job. Show motivation By saying movie star, astronaut or cat Breeder.

this Part is Boring. No offense

use prittier font Like comic sans

too much to read.

use pink ink to stand out.

thes skills aren't very good. you should Lie.

No stickers.

INTERVIEWS

The next step in getting a job is to go on a interview. This is when you talk to someone about yourself. Hear are some tips to help you get the job

SHOW UP LATE

This helps you look more important and like you have Better things to do.

DIRECT EYE CONTACT

Dont Blink OR look away. This shows that you're paying attention.

USE POSTERS

visual aids are very important. See next page for poster ideas.

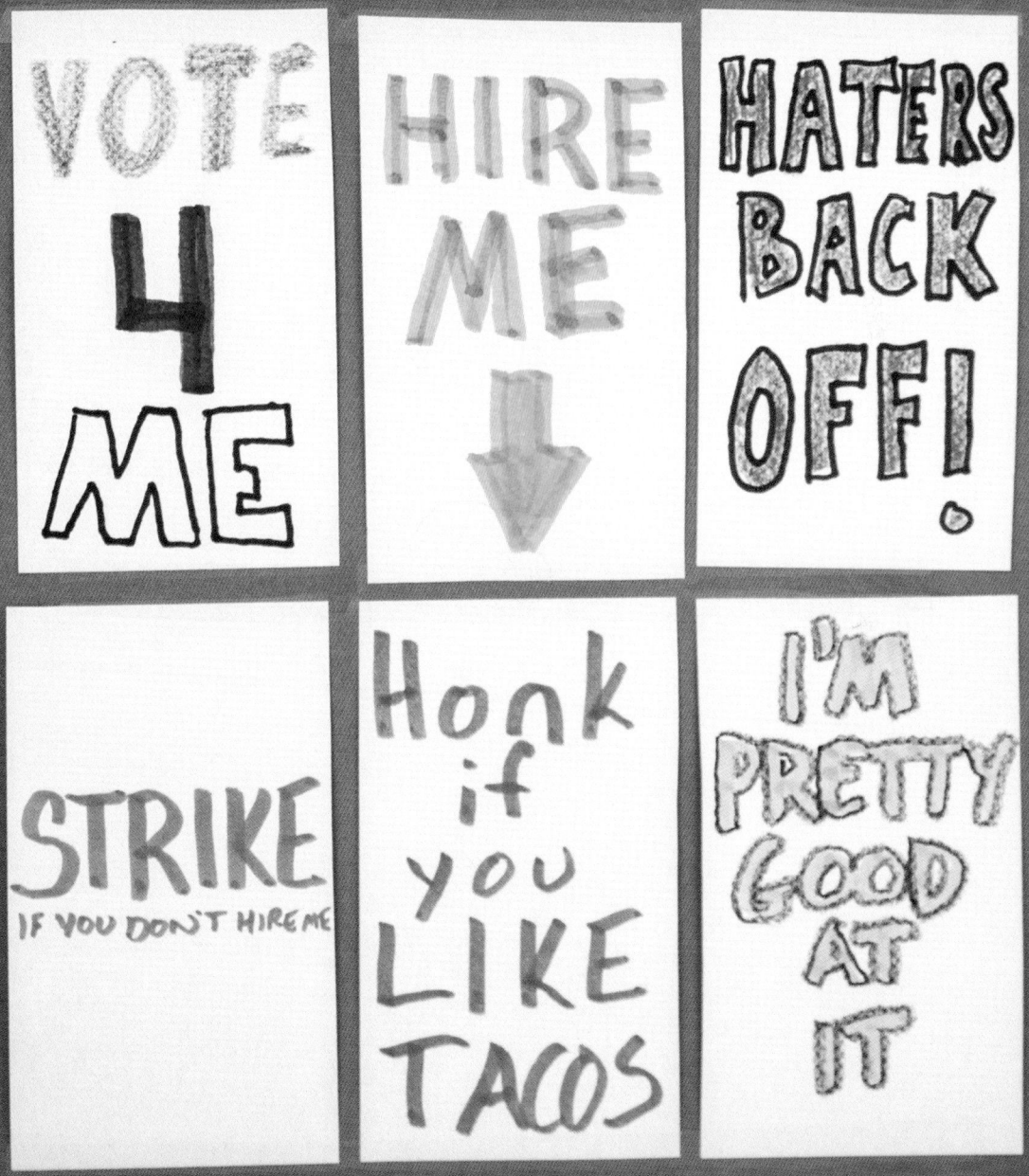
VOTE
4
ME
HIRE
ME
HATERS
BACK
OFF!
STRIKE
IF YOU DON'T HIRE ME
Honk
if
you
LIKE
TACOS
I'M
PRETTY
GOOD
AT
IT

INTERVIEW TIPS CONTINUED

DONT ANSWER ANY QUESTIONS

Beware of stranger Danger. ~~Remembe~~ remember you just met this person.

SING

Show you're talents. This is also good for when you dont know what to say.

PACK A SNACK

interviews can be long

COMPLIMENT THEM

see next page for compliment sugesstions

COMPLIMENTS

Your Breath smells delicious Like cheeseballs

Your long hairs cover almost all of your baldness

Looks Like you ate a big Lunch

your Forehead is very shiny

Scan this code to wach a sample interview video

Make Yourself Irreplaceable

UNPLUG all the telephones But your own.

Keep all the toilet paper in your office

Steal everyones lunch

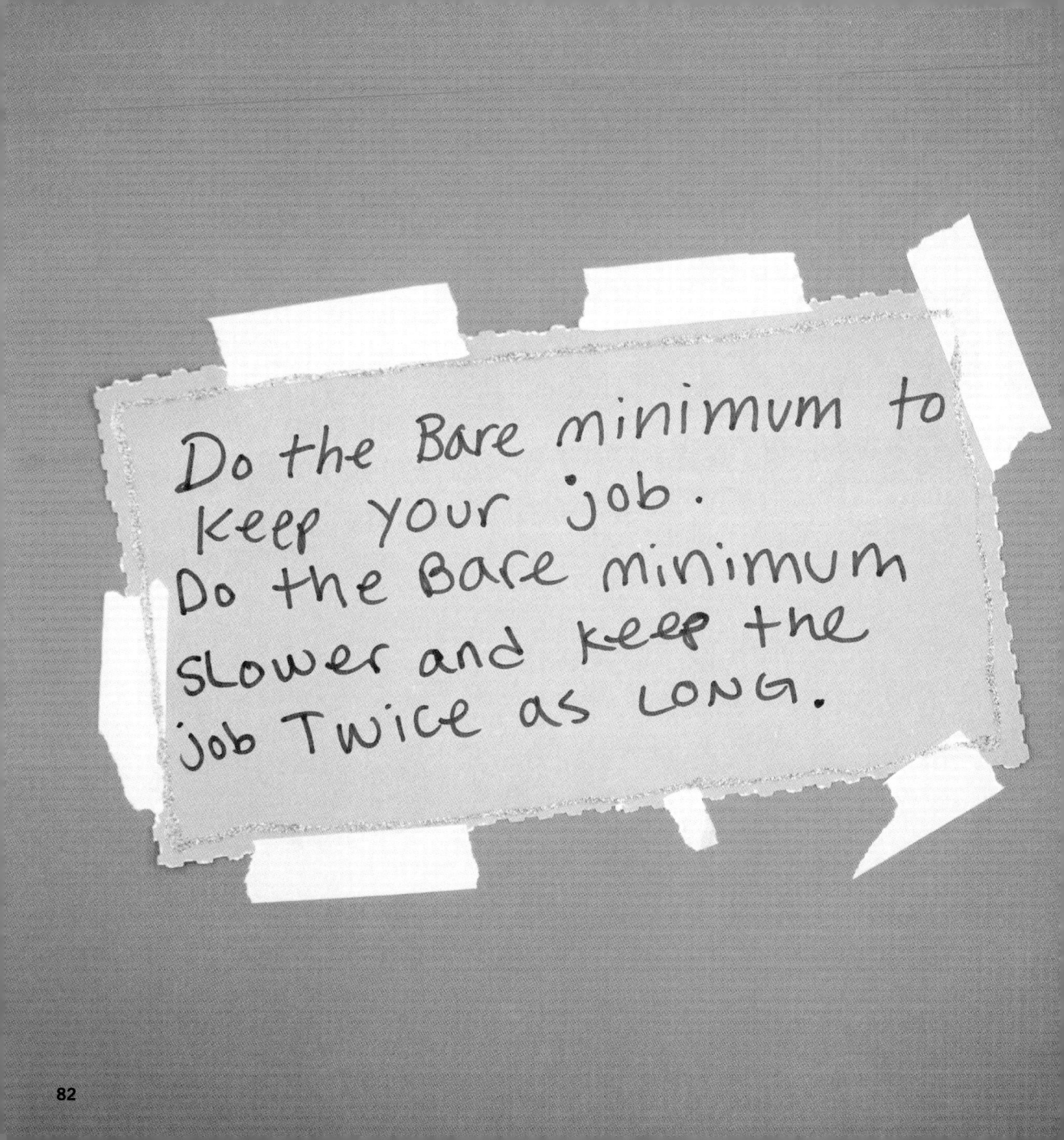
Do the Bare minimum to
keep your job.
Do the Bare minimum
slower and keep the
job Twice as LONG.

Massaging Boss
Look like im working
Eating
snacks
Resting eyes
Potty
work
Picking
Pie chart of my work DAY.

Work is Boring. Hear are some posters you can Blow up 2 stay motivated.

posters

Tape pieces of paper together to make a Big poster

example

JUMP

you might be a
WINNER
#1
you might not

Teamwork
a time to be
BETTER
than those
around you

Leadership
Obey ME!

Some Peo-
ple like
SPORTS

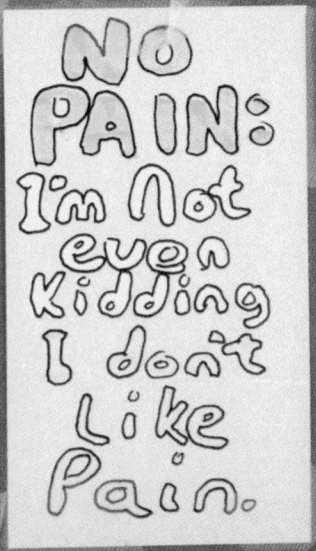
NO
PAIN:
I'm not
even
kidding
I don't
like
Pain.

GETTING Fired.

Tip 1: Never get fired.

Tip 2: Quit Before they fire you

Tip3: If they tell you you are Fired, dont Listen.

GETTING REVENGE

- Use the toilet paper you stole.
- De-friend them on social media.
- Never speak to them again.
- Get a new job. (go Back to page 1 of this chapter)
- [illegible]

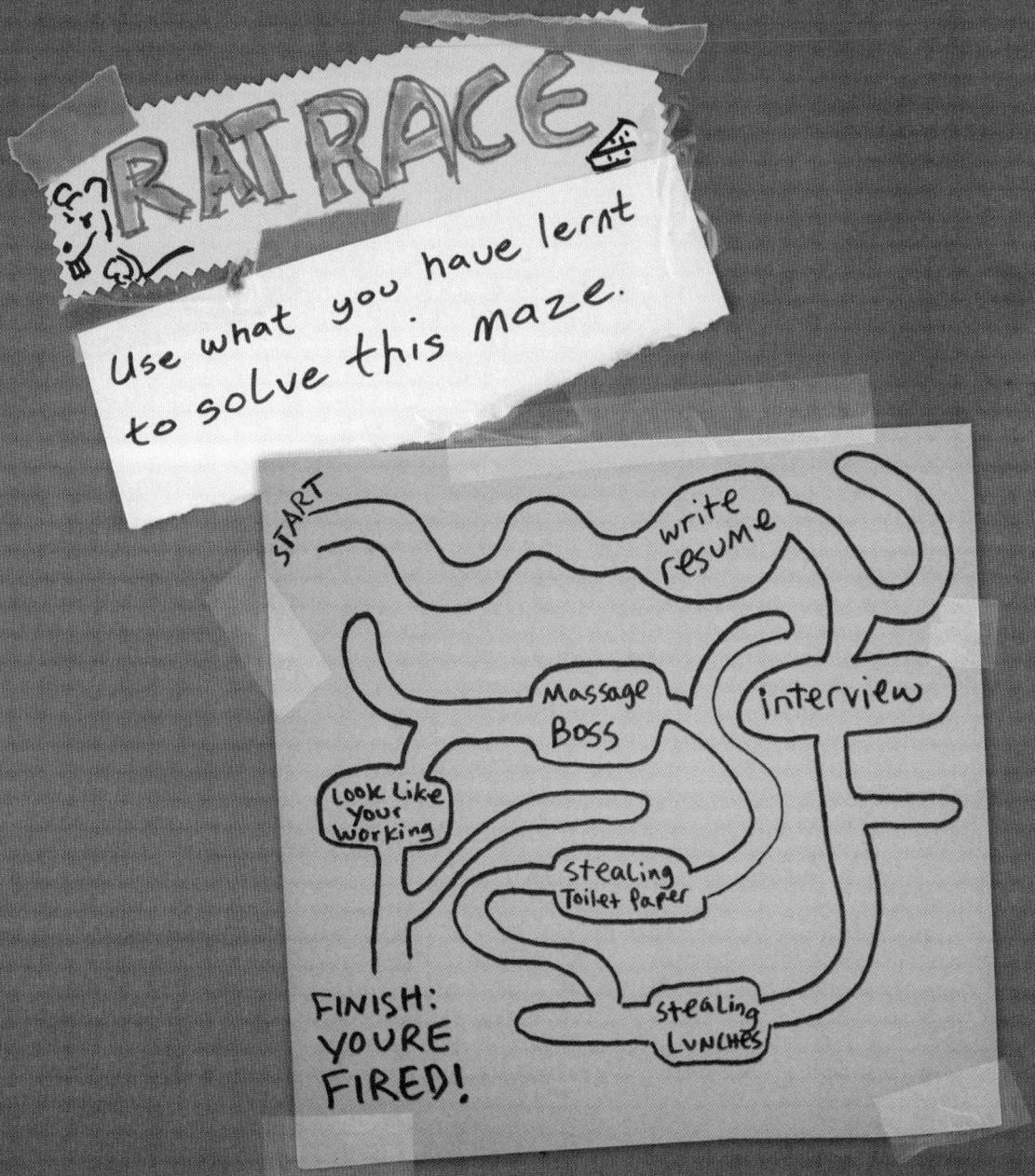
RATRACE
Use what you have lernt to solve this maze.
START
write resume
interview
Massage Boss
Look Like your working
stealing Toilet Paper
stealing LUNCHES
FINISH: YOURE FIRED!

FINANCE

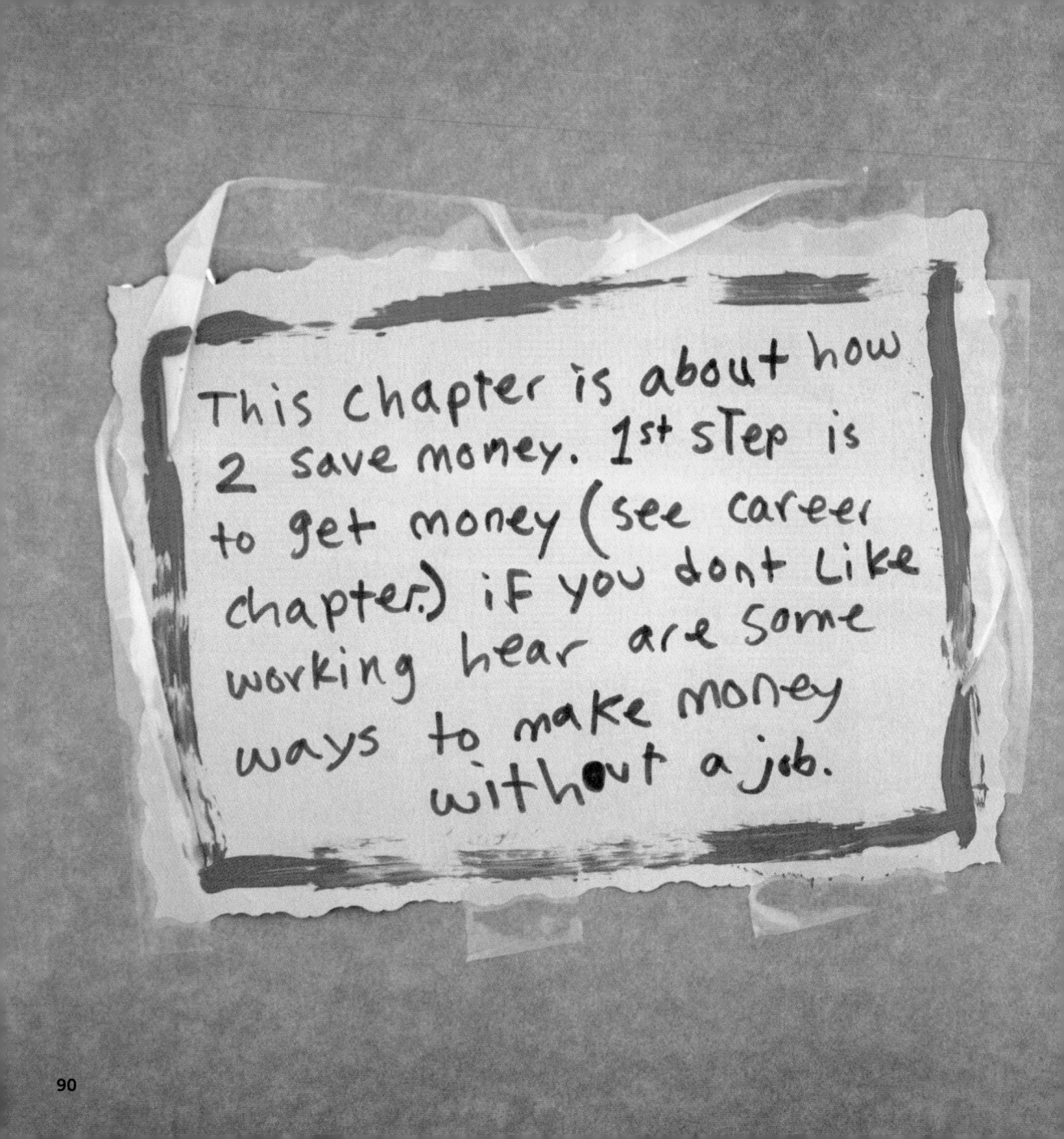
This chapter is about how
2 save money. 1st step is
to get money (see career
chapter.) if you dont like
working hear are some
ways to make money
without a job.

FIND IN COUCH

Extra Bonus! sometimes you find food.

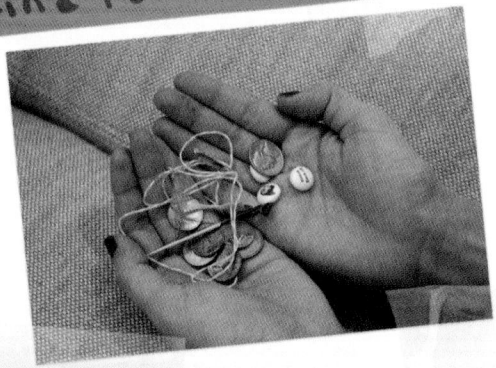

GET A RICH BAE.

make sure he is also famus.

ASK MOM

if she says no, find her purse and take it anyway.

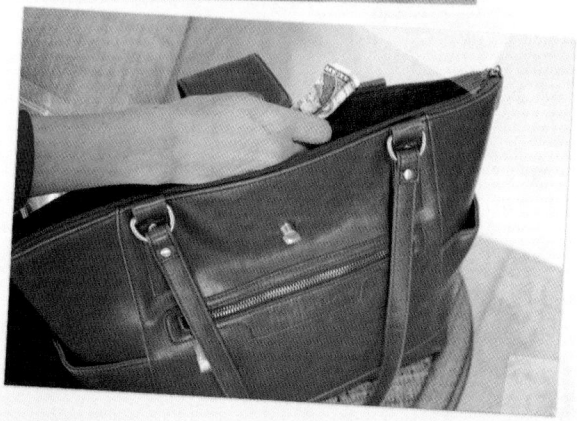

SELL STUFF

You can sell Broken or Boring Toys and stuff you made.

How to make MONEY
Another way to make money is to make money. You can use the examples on the next page and cut out you're very own money.

THE UNITED STATES OF MIRANDA
TACOMA
ONE DOLLAR

100
100
ONE HUNDRED BUCKS
100
100

10000
USA!
10000
ONE MILLEON
QUEEN MIRANDA
10000
ONE MILLEON DOLLARS
10000

IN MIRANDA WE TRUST
ONE
ONE DOLLAR
100 MIRANDA SINGS
100
100 ONE HUNDRED DOLARS
A MILLEON
MIRANDA SINGS
MY HOUSE

FINALLY
There is one way to get money without working, searching, dating, asking, cutting things out, or any of these kinds of things. You can actually get FREE MONEY. its using a little thing i like to call credit cards

SAVINGS
Places to hide your money
FRidge
Burry it
IN a poket
in a jar

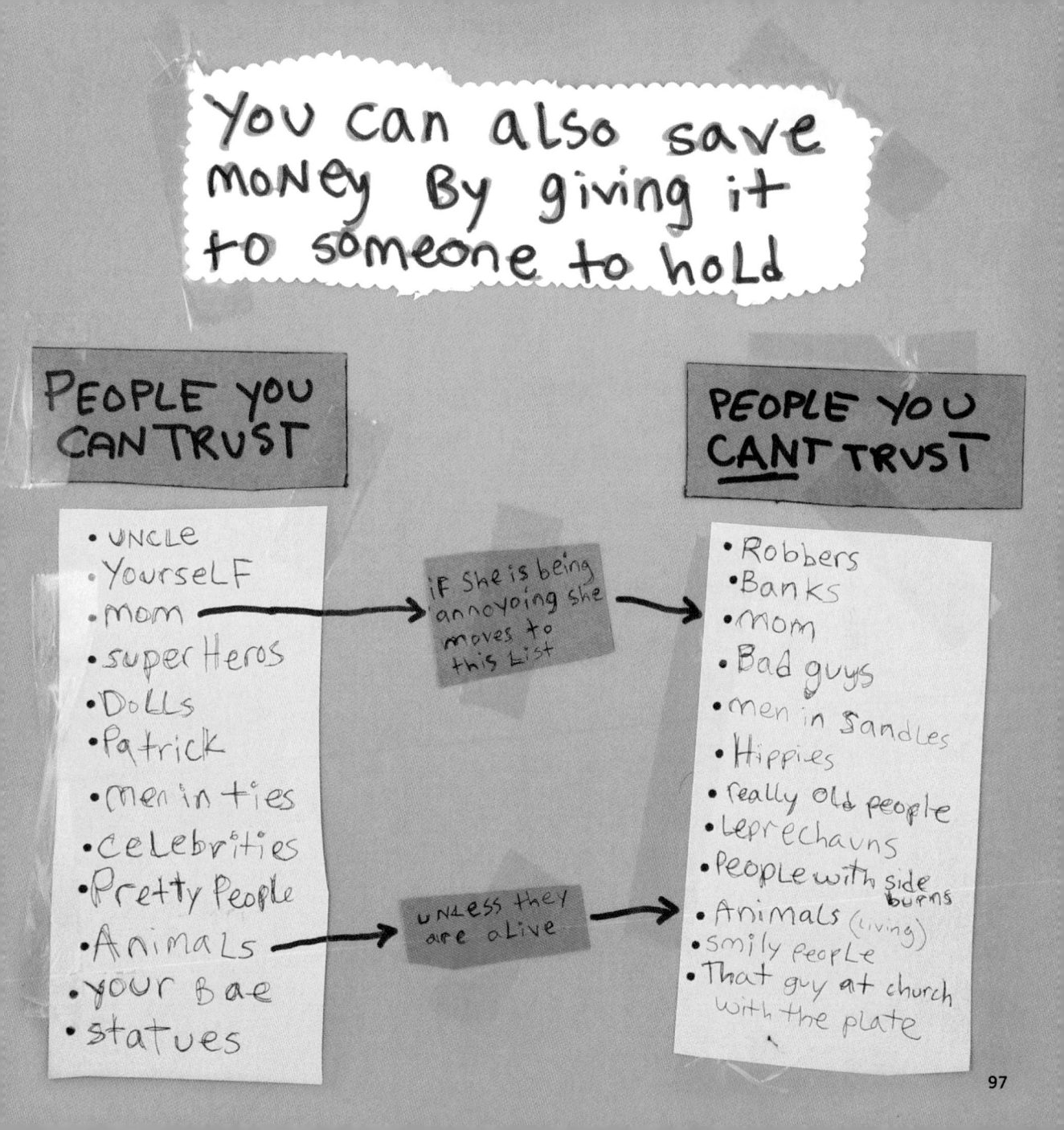
You can also save money By giving it to someone to hold
PEOPLE YOU CAN TRUST
• uncle
• Yourself
• mom
• superHeros
• Dolls
• Patrick
• men in ties
• celebrities
• Pretty People
• Animals
• your Bae
• statues
if She is being annoying she moves to this List
unless they are alive
PEOPLE YOU CANT TRUST
• Robbers
• Banks
• mom
• Bad guys
• men in Sandles
• Hippies
• really old people
• Leprechauns
• People with side burns
• Animals (living)
• smily people
• That guy at church with the plate

Investing

Here are a couple of good investments.

Bean Bag animals

- NEVER cut off the tags.
- if tags cam off, make new ones
- Play with often.

FOOD

- mostly Because it tasts good.
- Fun to hide and save 4 Later
- Extra Bonus: Kids meal toys

My uncle knows a lot about investing so he wrote this. so their you go.

I'M GLAD THAT YOU ASKED ABOUT THIS BECAUSE I HAVE JUST INVESTED IN AN OPPORTUNITY THAT YOU MIGHT BE INTERESTED IN ALSO. FOR JUST THE SMALL START-UP PRICE OF 179.99 YOU CAN BECOME A CONSULTANT AND SALES PERSON FOR THESE FANTASTIC VITAMINS.

BASICALLY IF YOU SIGN UP WITH ME TODAY, YOU'LL BE ABLE TO SELL VITAMINS FOR PROFIT AND YOU CAN RECRUIT NEW CONSULTANTS AND YOU'LL GET A PERCENTAGE OF THEIR SALES. I GET A PERCENTAGE OF YOUR SALES JUST LIKE THE GUY WHO RECRUITED ME GETS A PERCENTAGE OF MY SALES

IN FACT IF YOUR RECRUITS GET NEW RECRUITS YOU GET A PERCENTAGE OF THEIR SALES. AND SO ON, AND SO ON. EVERYBODY MAKES MONEY TOGETHER! SOUNDS GREAT, RIGHT?

I KNOW WHAT YOU'RE THINKING, "JIM, THIS SOUNDS LIKE JUST ANOTHER PYRAMID SCHEME." WHAT? NO. WORKS COMPLETELY DIFFERENT. I'LL DRAW A DIAGRAM TO MAKE IT MORE CLEAR.

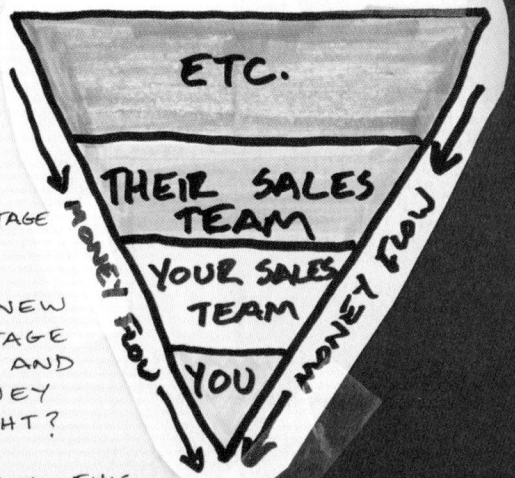

Look out for good Deals

COUPONS

CUT out these coupons To use

30% OFF TOYS

½ off Lipstick

Free Cat!

Extra meat when buying meat

Buy 1 Get 3 Sodas

Name your Price

wach out 4
these jips
REFILLS ARE 50¢
JIP
JIP
New Bag of Chips
JIP
TOTAL JIP

Making Money Grow

A lot of people talk about making money grow. They are liars. I've tried it and it doesn't work at all.

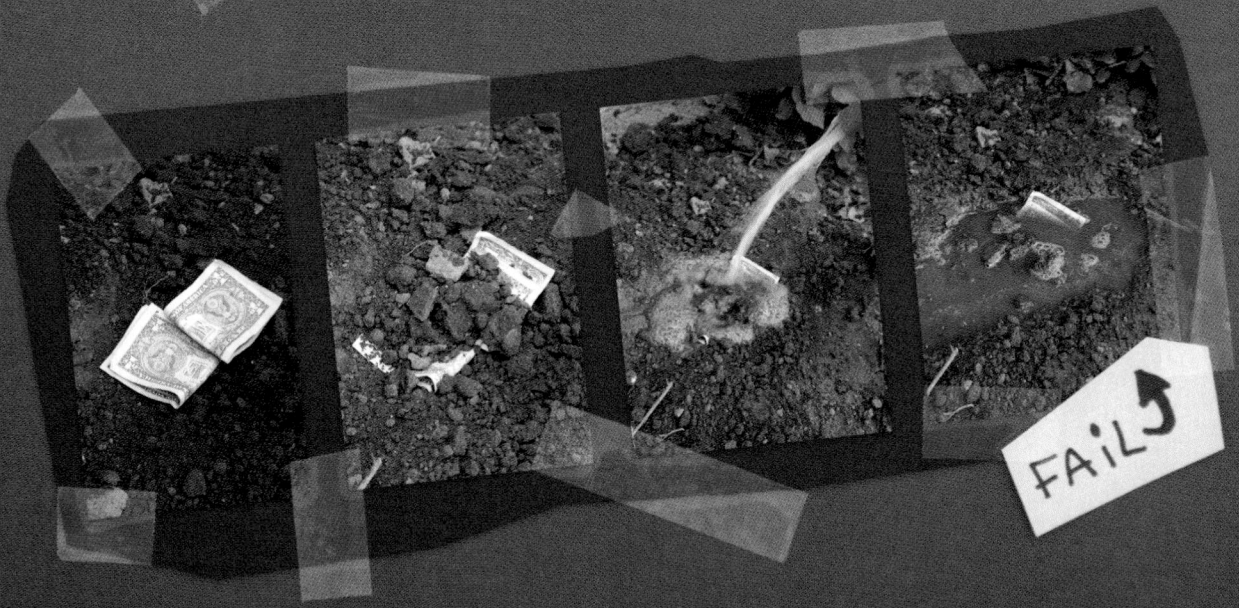

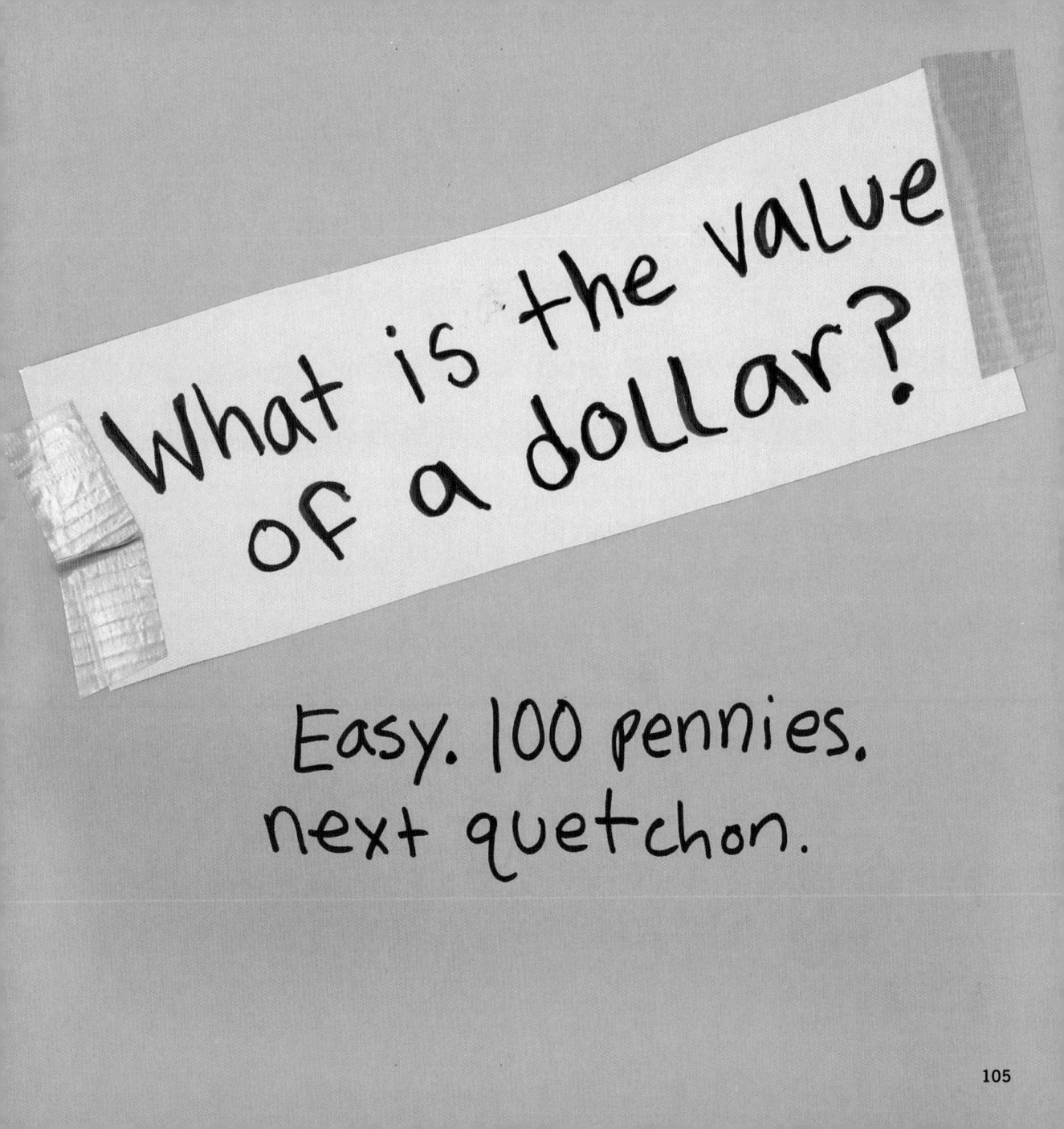
What is the value of a dollar?
Easy. 100 pennies. next quetchon.

TRY some of these Free activities

Go to the pound

its like the zoo but Free and Better cuz they change out the animals every week

Birthday party

Find a Birthday Party at a park. They dont know you so they wont expect a present. Free cake. Free Food. Free jumpy house. Free Pinyata.

wach TV

Doesnt cost anything and you can turn it up loud enough so you cant hear your mom telling you wat to do.

Road trip

Flying is so espensive so just trick someone into driving you anywhear you want. its Fun and Free

WHAT CAN YOU GET

This is a dollar. and it can buy you things Like tacos or

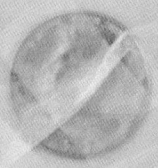

i never seen one of these they probly dont even exist

This is good to get bouncy Balls or gum.

Tip For waiter

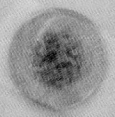

This coin is ~~too~~ Fat for how much its worth.

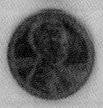

Pointless. throw away.

Other uses For money

Fix a wiggly table

Cleaning out teeth

A top (perfect toy for Babys)

writing a note.

LeTs PLay A gamE

connect the dots!

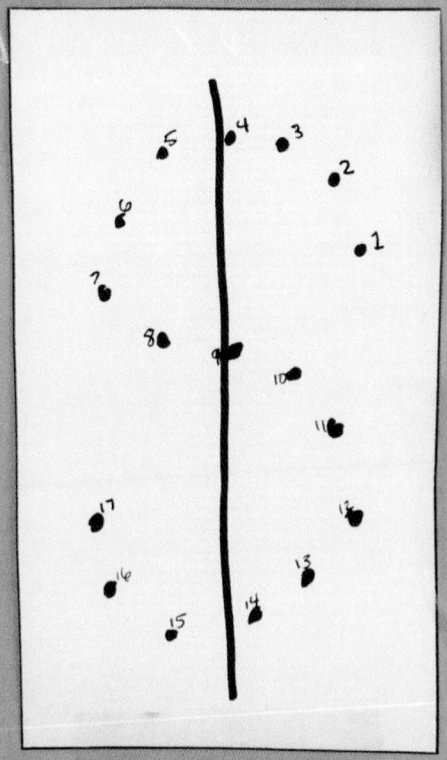

its a mystery...

What could it Be?

HINTS

① it has to do with this chapter
② its the symbol 4 money
③ its a "5" with a line through it.

Hidden Pictures

Find the hidden money just like in real life!

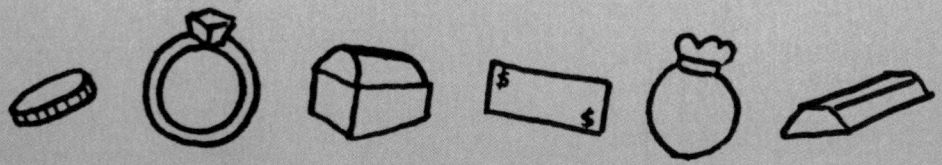

SMART

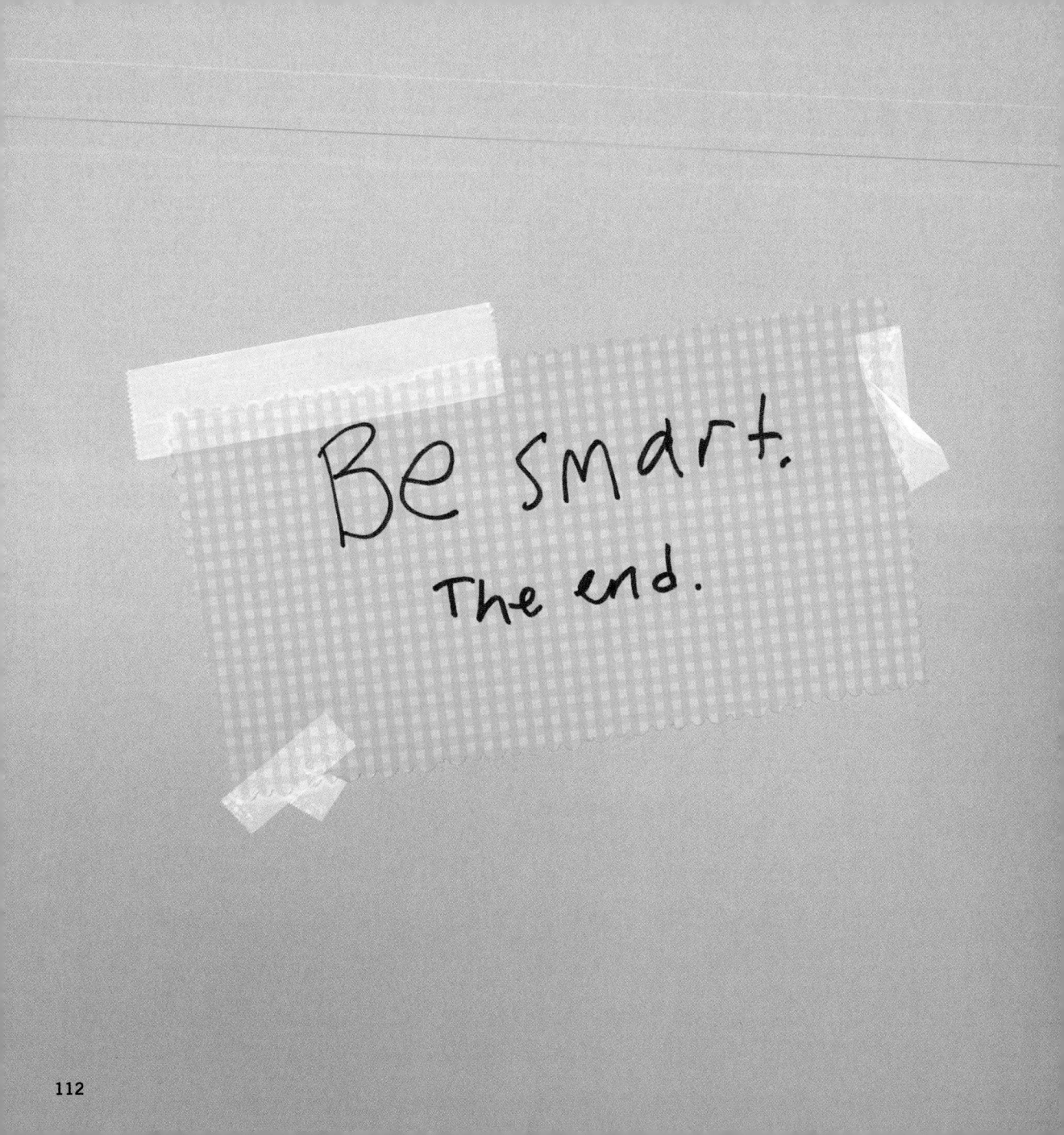
Be smart.
The end.

INTERNET

its important to have the skill of the internet cuz everything on the internet is true. Come with me as i unfold how 2 internet the best.

Before you get started online you need to learn to speak the language.

LOL - laugh out loud
WERK - to werk
selfie - a pitchur
Yolo - You only live once
OMG - Oh my ~~gracias~~ ~~gratious~~ ~~gracius~~ gracias
FML = fogrot my lunch
LMAO - let me ask others
BAE - (See piture 1)
FAIL - Falling And Internet Laughter
ILYSM - i love yogurt sometimes
gr8 - growling and 8

Piture 1

Social Media

social media is a great place to take pitchurs of your food, poke people, make people jealis, and brag. *see exampels below*

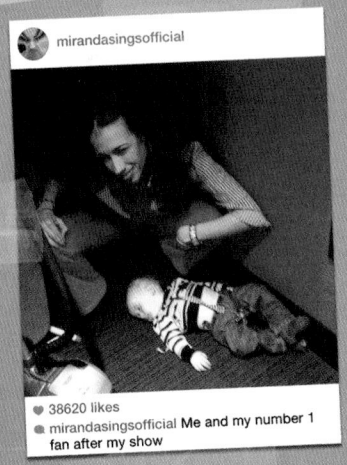

Miranda Sings
@MirandaSings

I always new I was famous because people look at me some times.

Miranda Sings
Posted by Miranda Sings

hi

13,434 Likes · 1,068 Comments

Like Comment Share

Miranda Sings
@MirandaSings

I'm so glad I've changed so many lives. #blessed #livingTheDeeam #famous #Obamacare

Social Media Platforms

My stupid Lawyer said i cant put actual names of social medias in my Book. so i disguised their names so you wont know wich is wich.

Blitter - For Fangirling & hashtagging

Bluetube For people to get Famous

Blinstagram - For showing your food and Face.

Blacebook - For old people

Blapchat - For pitchurs that need to disappear (poo, panties, strangers,)

Bline - For videos you want to wach over and over and over and over

Blumber - i dont get it.

Video Ideas

CHALLENGES

it doesnt matter what the challenge is. it will get views. so eat a spider, burn off your hairs, take a slushi Bath, something respecktable like that. People like waching you throw up. Almost dying is Better.

TUTORIALS

Teach People how to do something online cuz obviously your opinion is more valuble then Professionals @ things like fashon and cooking

COLLABORATIONS

Take advantage of other youtubers By making videos with them and stealing their subscribers

MUSIC VIDEOS

Sing a cover of someone elses song. This is grs Because you dont have to Be talented or creative. just do it & people will watch

Tips for going viral.

CLEAN

Before

After

use good Liting.

Viral Videos.

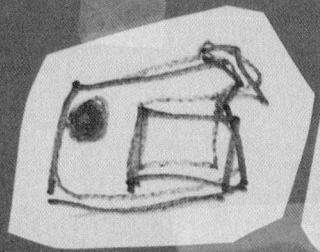

Camera

Computer

Person

Snack

WHAT YOU NEED

viral videos are videos that spread relly fast. Like warts.

viral videos I made

Voice Lesson

California Girls

Do You want to Build a snowman

Taking pitchurs and putting them online is very important. The better you look, the more likes you will get. Just like in real life.

Things you can Post to BL Instagram

Face

Food

Animals

Shoes

Coffee

Quotes

A selfie is a pitchur of yourself or other things
good Angles
UNDER
OVER
FRONT
FACE
Phone
Aim
Extend
Person (you)

TAKE SelFies with Thing S.

Animals

Jesus

Mirrors

Food

other

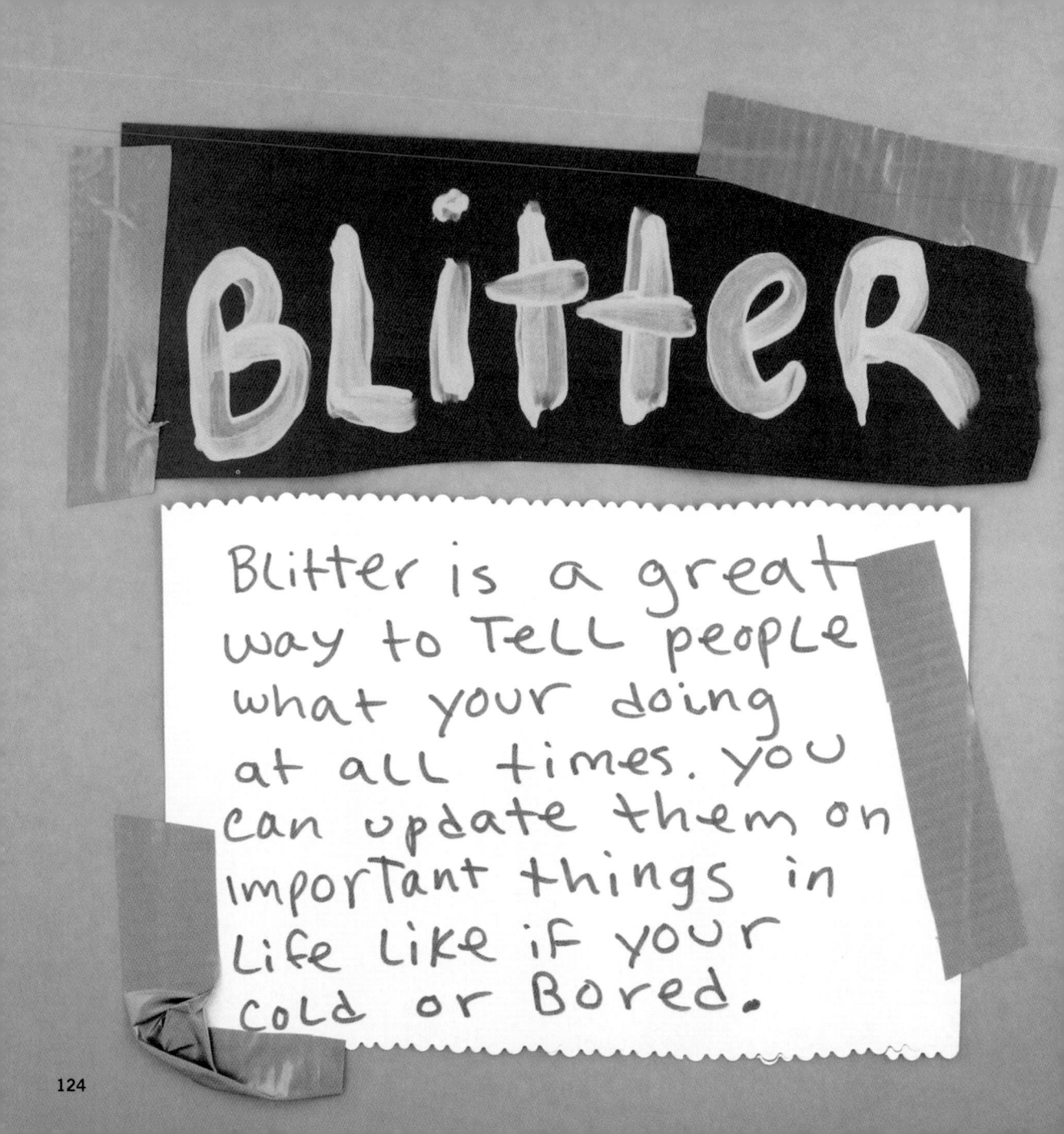
BLitteR
Blitter is a great way to Tell people what your doing at all times. you can update them on important things in Life Like if your cold or Bored.

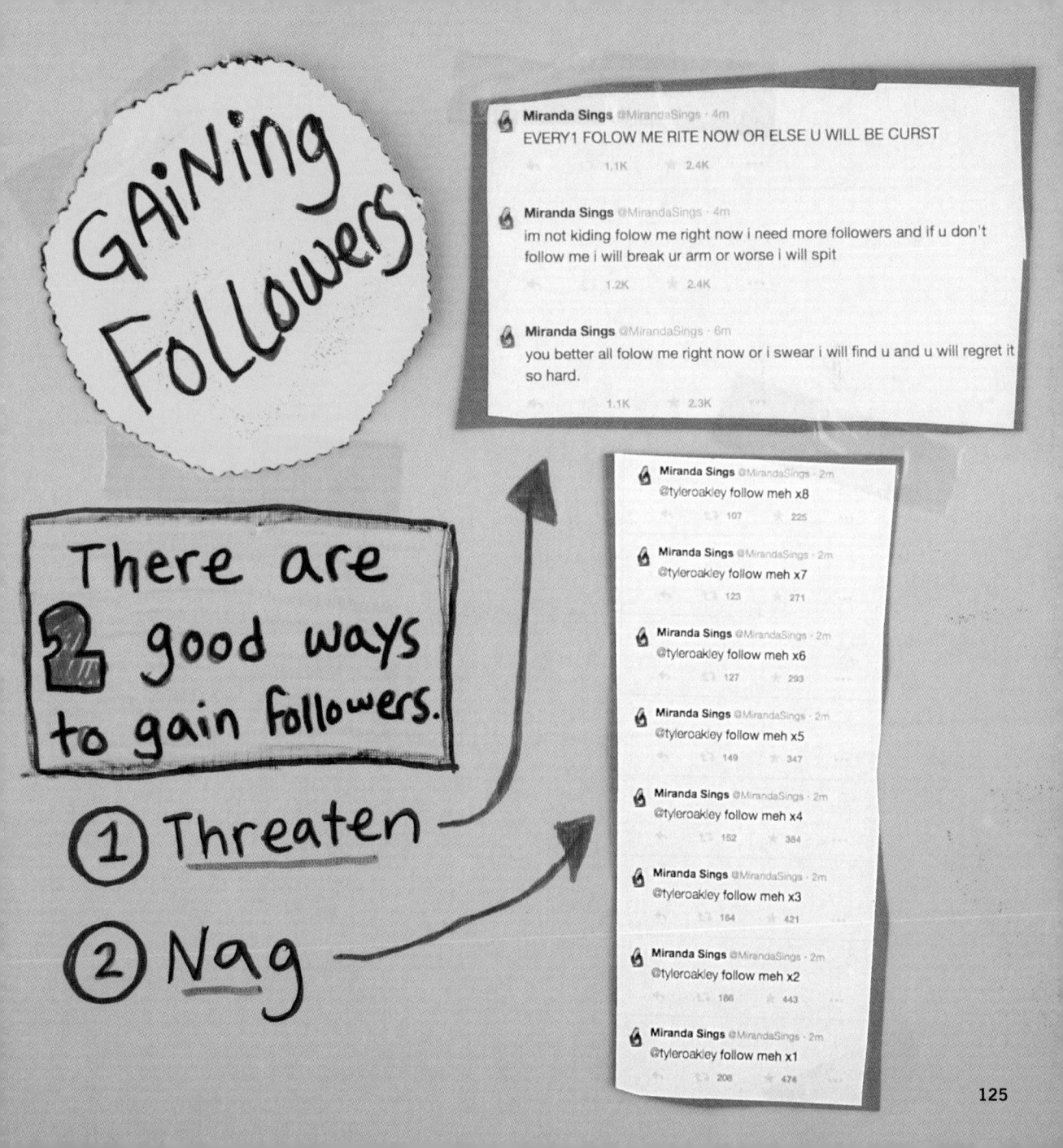
Gaining Followers
Miranda Sings @MirandaSings · 4m
EVERY1 FOLOW ME RITE NOW OR ELSE U WILL BE CURST
1.1K 2.4K
Miranda Sings @MirandaSings · 4m
im not kiding folow me right now i need more followers and if u don't follow me i will break ur arm or worse i will spit
1.2K 2.4K
Miranda Sings @MirandaSings · 6m
you better all folow me right now or i swear i will find u and u will regret it so hard.
1.1K 2.3K
There are 2 good ways to gain followers.
1 Threaten
2 Nag
Miranda Sings @MirandaSings · 2m
@tyleroakley follow meh x8
107 225
Miranda Sings @MirandaSings · 2m
@tyleroakley follow meh x7
123 271
Miranda Sings @MirandaSings · 2m
@tyleroakley follow meh x6
127 293
Miranda Sings @MirandaSings · 2m
@tyleroakley follow meh x5
149 347
Miranda Sings @MirandaSings · 2m
@tyleroakley follow meh x4
152 384
Miranda Sings @MirandaSings · 2m
@tyleroakley follow meh x3
164 421
Miranda Sings @MirandaSings · 2m
@tyleroakley follow meh x2
186 443
Miranda Sings @MirandaSings · 2m
@tyleroakley follow meh x1
208 474

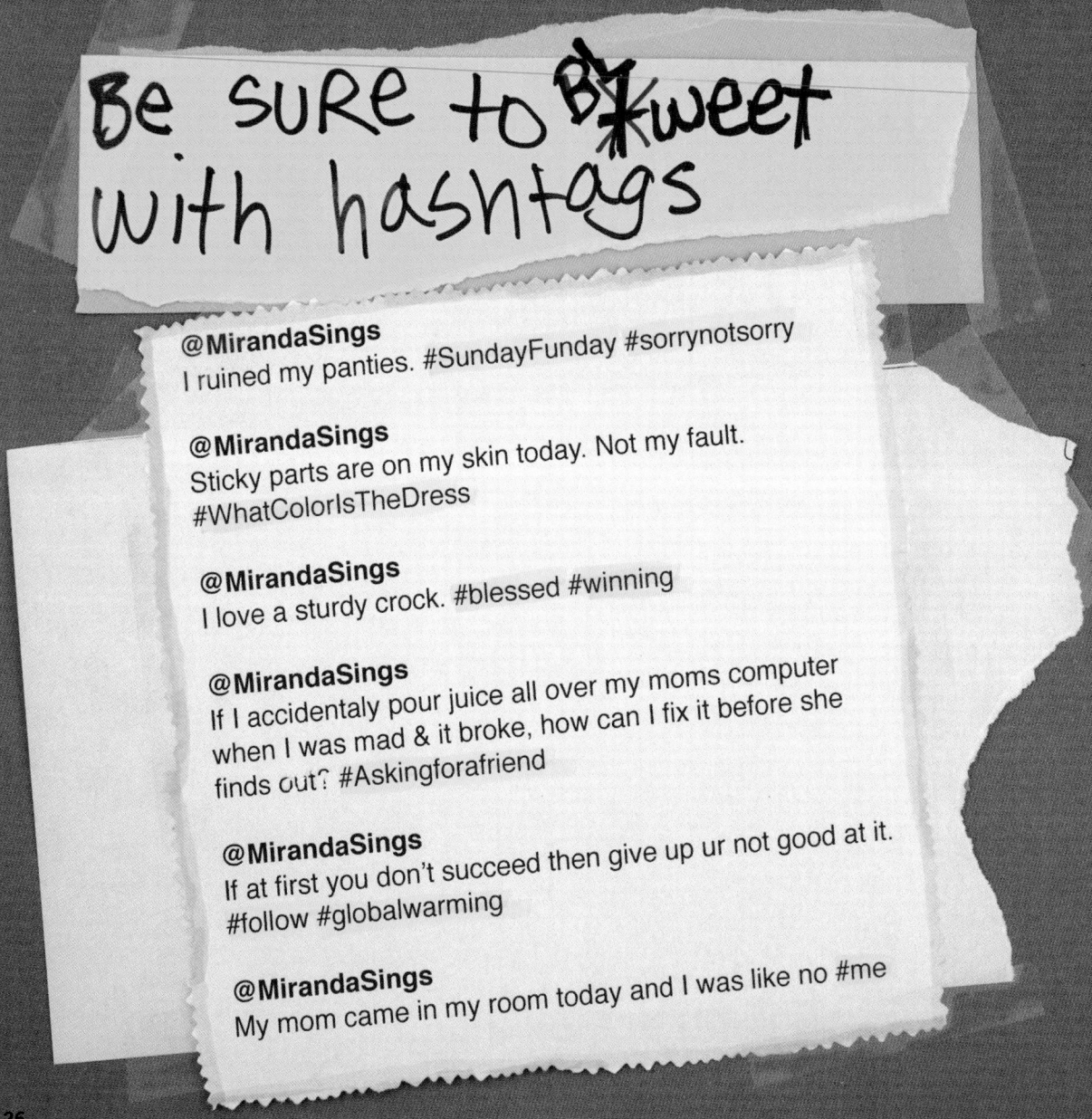
Be sure to Bitweet
with hashtags
@MirandaSings
I ruined my panties. #SundayFunday #sorrynotsorry
@MirandaSings
Sticky parts are on my skin today. Not my fault.
#WhatColorIsTheDress
@MirandaSings
I love a sturdy crock. #blessed #winning
@MirandaSings
If I accidentaly pour juice all over my moms computer
when I was mad & it broke, how can I fix it before she
finds out? #Askingforafriend
@MirandaSings
If at first you don't succeed then give up ur not good at it.
#follow #globalwarming
@MirandaSings
My mom came in my room today and I was like no #me

Hashtags are used to explain your pitchur. Also to brag.
#MYSELF
#YOLO
#Blessed
#Kony 2012
#MadAtMyUncle

Blacebook
My mom and uncle use
Blacebook all the time
So im going to let them
write a few things.
They Better Not Be boring
or annoying or i wont let
them in the Book im not even
kidding.

I love Bacebook. it's a great place to connect with old friends from grade school and say happy Birthday to people. I also really enjoy being poked.

Martha posted a lovely photo of a kitten on my face wall last week and Ruby wrote a comment on it that was simply hilarious. Did you see that? I cant remember what it said now... something about cats I think. I remember it ended with "lol" or something clever like that.

Bacebook is also a great place to create events and start group messages about upcoming craft parties. Although, Ruby wasn't invited to Lisa's scrabble event last week. I hope she is doing well after that. Everyone loves my posts about Miranda. Yesterday I was given 3 likes and 5 pokes! Such fun! ♡ ~Bethany

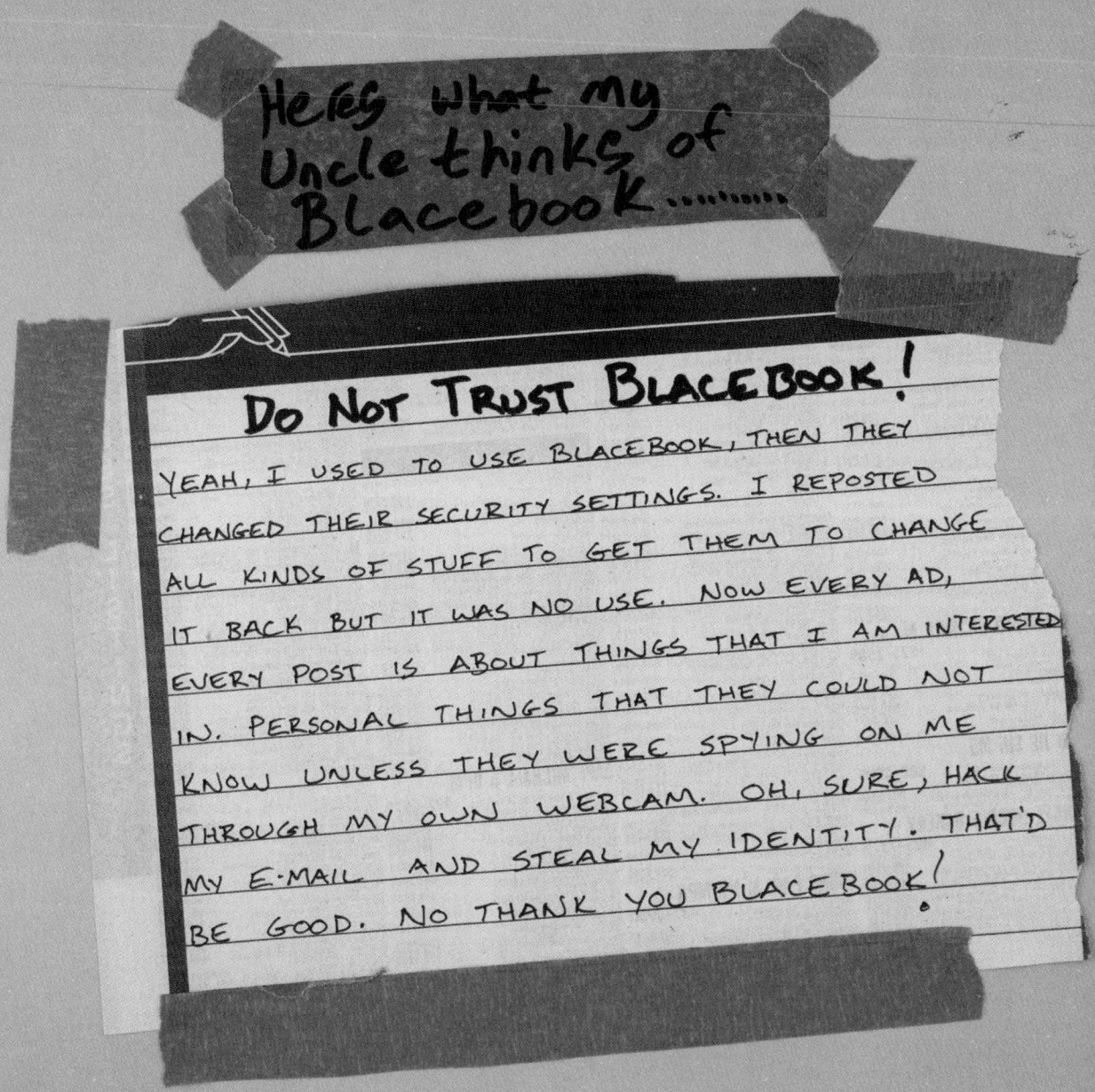
Here's what my Uncle thinks of Blacebook.....
DO NOT TRUST BLACEBOOK!
YEAH, I USED TO USE BLACEBOOK, THEN THEY CHANGED THEIR SECURITY SETTINGS. I REPOSTED ALL KINDS OF STUFF TO GET THEM TO CHANGE IT BACK BUT IT WAS NO USE. NOW EVERY AD, EVERY POST IS ABOUT THINGS THAT I AM INTERESTED IN. PERSONAL THINGS THAT THEY COULD NOT KNOW UNLESS THEY WERE SPYING ON ME THROUGH MY OWN WEBCAM. OH, SURE, HACK MY E-MAIL AND STEAL MY IDENTITY. THAT'D BE GOOD. NO THANK YOU BLACEBOOK!

BLapchat

i Love this Social medid cuz you can try out new hairstyles and Looks.

AND if you take a pic of something you dont Like it disappears! heres a example of a pitchur im glad Disappeared

Bline
Bline is a place
where you scream a
Lot, say Bad words, or
Be rasist. i choose to
Scream. what do you choose?
circle one...
SCREAM
BAD WORDS
RASIST

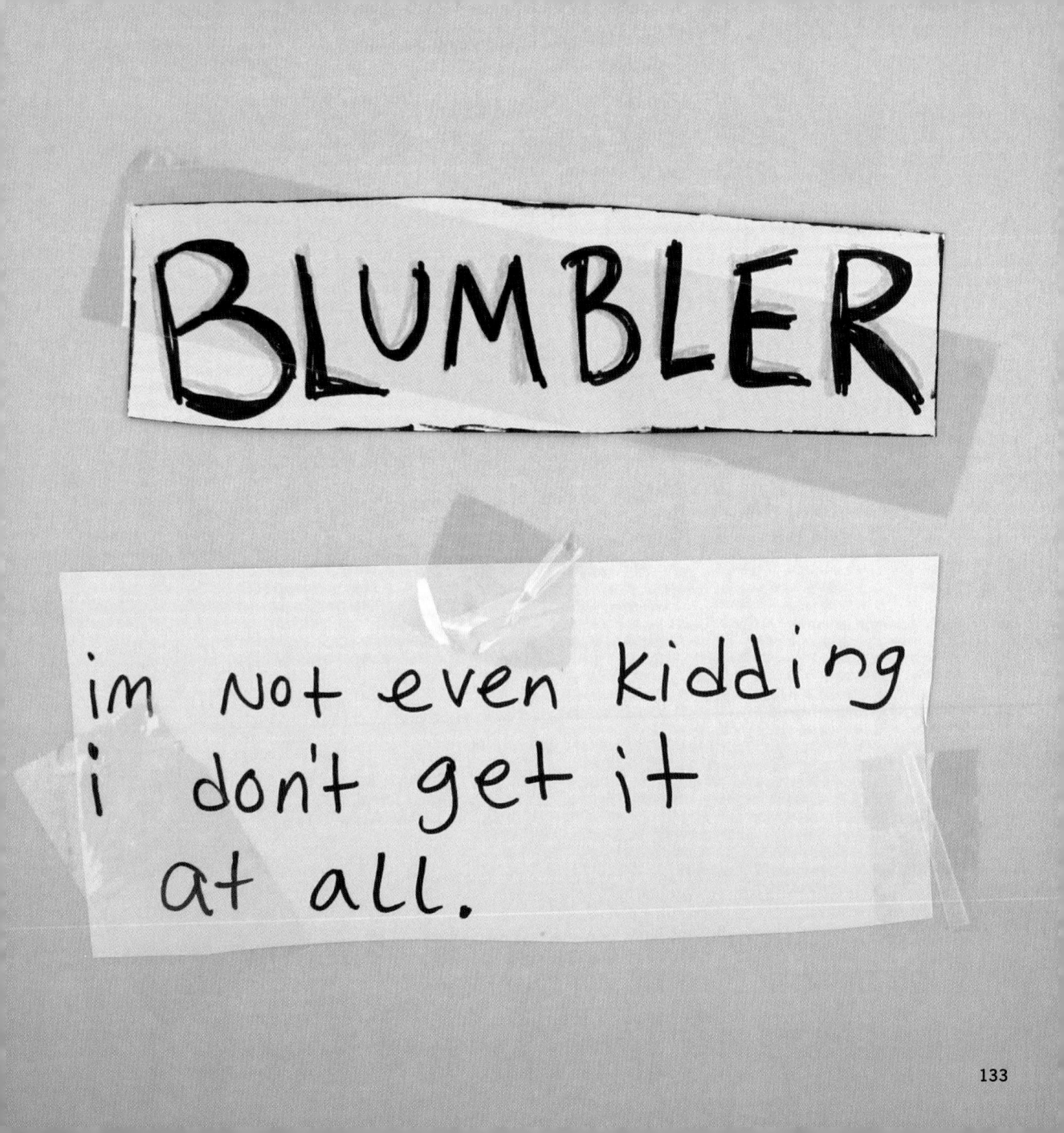
BLUMBLER
im not even kidding
i don't get it
at all.

HAtemaiL

Hatemail is something you will get from Haters on your social medias. its relly rude and ANOYING. the next few pages are hatemaiLs i have gotted on my social medias.
(close eyes while reading. its very dangerus.)

HATEmail

MisterGolwin MD
well now my ears have aids

Kristorgyles1982
The entire video I was wondering how she was covering her monster size penis

dontstepbeleevn5
no, ' no no no no.....STOP SINGING LISTEN TO YOURSELF AND COMPARE IT TO REAL SINGERS U SOND LIKE UR POOING!!!!!!!!!!!!

f1oridatrou6lemkr
BEEP YOU MIRDANA

Poppxd4ddy
She's uglier than he'll

MsSupTe55o
Thumbs up if you only clicked on this video because you thought she was going to chocck :)

HATEMAIL

xxxgothicks69
I had to stab myself with a pencil to dull the pain this video gave me

he110kewlgang42
wwwww is this botch beep im fur real? Nasty get the beep away from this kids you look like some retraded rapest and u sing like beep! If i ever see this hoe beep retard ima knock you out smash your face in that sand and stomp on your head till u shut the beep up for good that was so bad i couldn't even listen to the whole thing!
Sad face… my ear r burned

InsameMasheen5
Oh, I'm sorry, I couldn't hear you over the sound of me puking

mik mccornix
uhygtykbjvycryfdxefgxdrgerfgftcr5yfr5hfrr4t5 beep you go to hell and stay there forever

HATEMAIL

Ma661Nawly
What the beep you tryna do to people dread? You in some kinda beep in mad people home Iowa? LAWD HAVE MERCY..... GIRL HUSH YOUR BLASTE MOUTH NAW..... setups....only squak squak squak squak you a beep parrot....HUSH!

Ch1po4u5
My dad came in and I switched to porn because it was easier to explain

pr1nce55pa9s
seriously wot is rong wiv ur lip? and wot is rong wiv ur voice? u need to sort urself out and get a life, i am NOT a hater coz u make me and my family laugh our heads off. but if we r goin by talent, i do hate ya, i am a hater! stop postin these videos and just do sumink else!! ur ruining my life!!

Re5pectab1eBeeuTay
1st of you can't sing, nor like a black woman. You don't have to be big to sing like a bigger black women. you cant sing so stop. And your stupid cause black woman don't move their head, it's called having soul, which you will never have. This answer is from a serious woman (a serious and now angry black woman) unlike you.

WORD Search

A X B C R B F A R I T W
Y N R A G L A H O L E E
B O B F T A I C H Y E T
K M L E G W L X A A T X
L M A O # B L E S S E D
O W T F A R T E H O G I
L E T M S B J K T M R C
P O Y L S E F A A G 8 K
S E L F I E R Y G N O Y

WORDS to find

BRB	WTF	FAIL	#BLESSED	NO
YOLO	BRB	SELFIE	HASHTAG	GR8
LOL	TTYL	LMAO	ILY	
GTG	JK	FML	OMG	

HEALTH

What is health?

Oh i'm glad you asked. Health is being healthy. like not being sick or jumping jacks--all these kinds of things.

Your body is a temple also it is skin and hair. So Just saying you have to take care of it.

In this chapter i will explane the importnance of exersize, eating rite and getting a good nights rest.

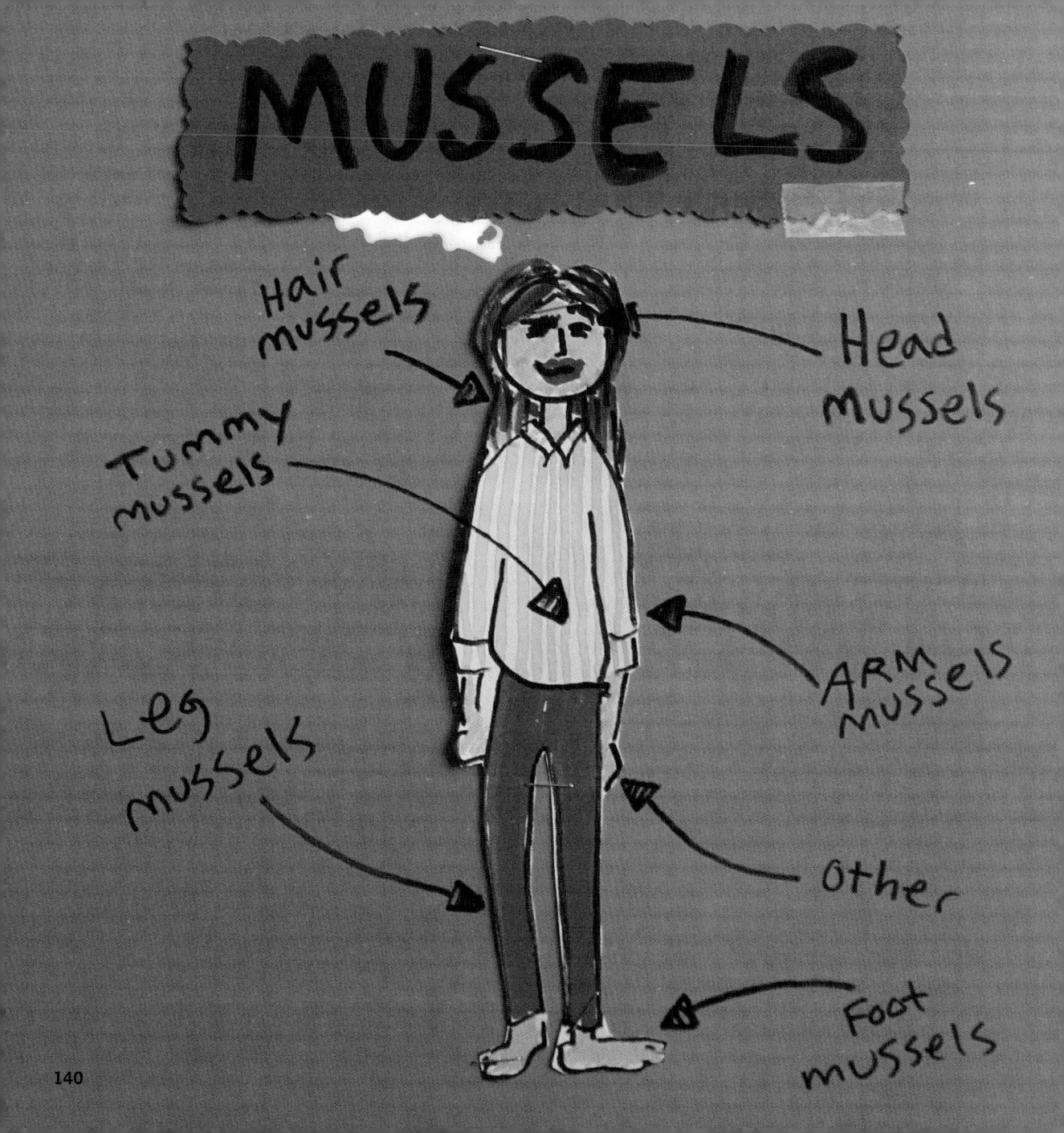
MUSSELS
Hair mussels
Head mussels
Tummy mussels
ARM mussels
Leg mussels
Other
Foot mussels

Dont Pull a musle when you exersize. Always Strench first.

Tummy Strenches!

Face etsersize

Arm exersize

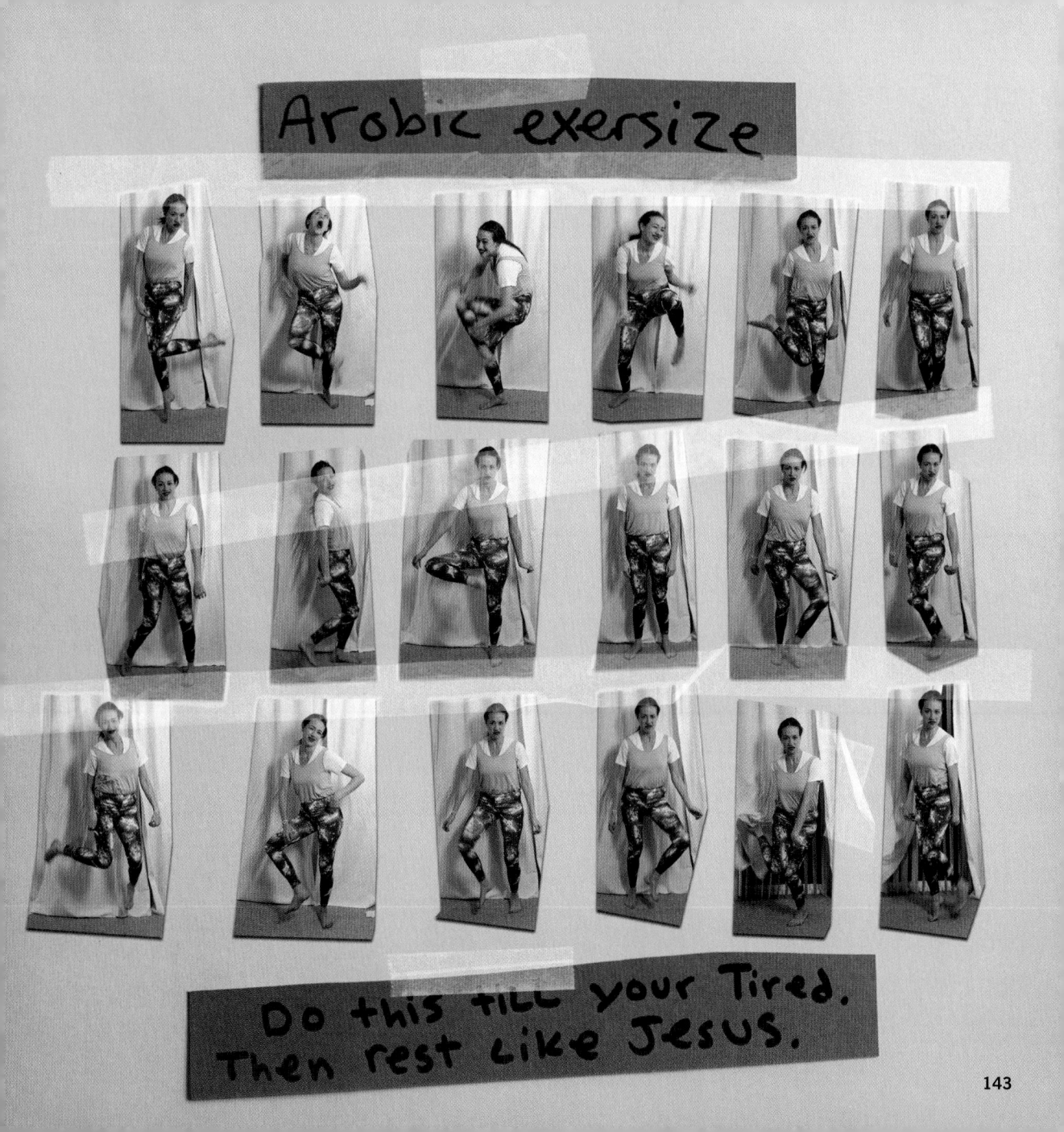
Arobic exersize
Do this till your Tired.
Then rest like Jesus.

you are what you
put in you so choose
what you put in
wisely. you wouldn't
want to get sick...
or worse - gag.

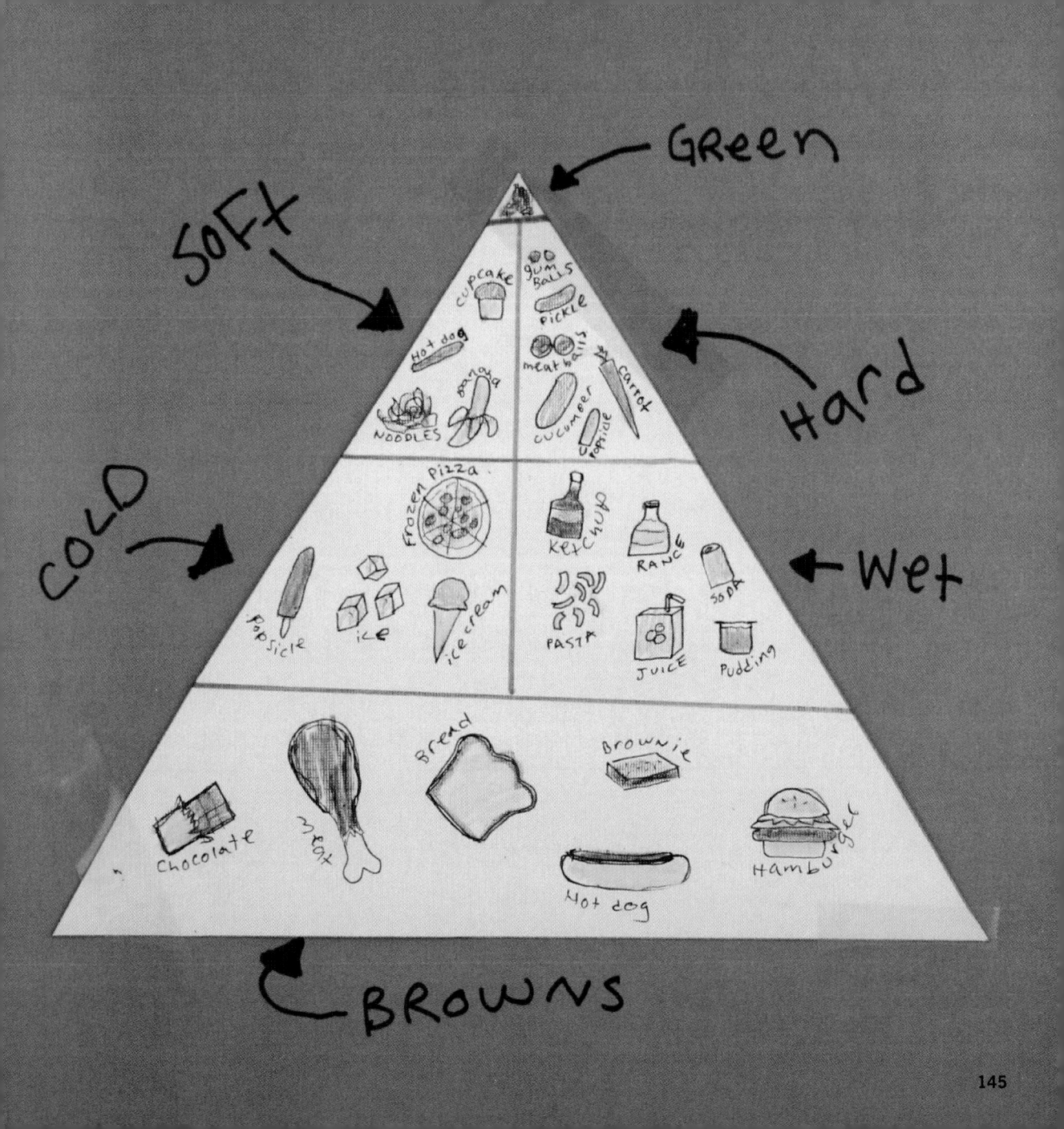
GREEN
SOFT
HARD
COLD
WET
BROWNS
cupcake
gum balls
pickle
Hot dog
meat balls
carrot
banana
NOODLES
cucumber
popsicle
Pizza
frozen
ketchup
RANCH
SOAP
popsicle
ice
ice cream
PASTA
JUICE
Pudding
Chocolate
meat
bread
brownie
Hamburger
Hot dog

The Best Meals
have cheese Folds.

RECIPES FOR EATING

SPAGETIOS

1. Have ur uncle open the can
2. Heat it up
3. or dont
4. i like it better warmed up.
5. Put in Bowl
6. get a spoon
7. dip spoon in Bowl
8. Pick spoon up. (it will be heavier so wach out)
9. Chew it but not too much because its fun too swallow the whole "O"s.
10. Swallow
11. Finish eating
12. put bowl in sink
13. Find any O's that fell on the ground and eat.
14. Yell to mom

Mac n Cheese

1. make mac N cheese
2. ~~Put in Hot dogs~~
3. Eat it
4. repeet.

Couldnt find a pitchur of mac n cheese so i used this pic instead

Ambrosia

this is one of Miranda's favorite meals. Hear is my special recipe. Please try it and send me photos at Betharysings874291z@gmail.com.

INGREDIENTS

* JELLO
* CANNED FRUIT
* WHIPPED TOPPING
* RAISENS
* MARSHMALLOWS
* CORN
* MEAT (OPTIONAL)

DIRECTIONS

1. make the jello
2. add fruit, raisens, marshmallows, corn, and meat.
3. put in fridge over night and then add whipped topping.

More Recipes
HOT DOG
Microwave hot Dod
TUNA SALAD
Put BOth in Bag. squeez in mouth.

Dont eat greens.
PLants give us oxygin
if you eat them we
will sufficate. save
the earth. Dont eat
PLants.
Dont Eat.

Eat your Browns
everyone likes good
strong meets inside
them. it makes you
Big and helthy. Also
it tastes good.

Eat it.

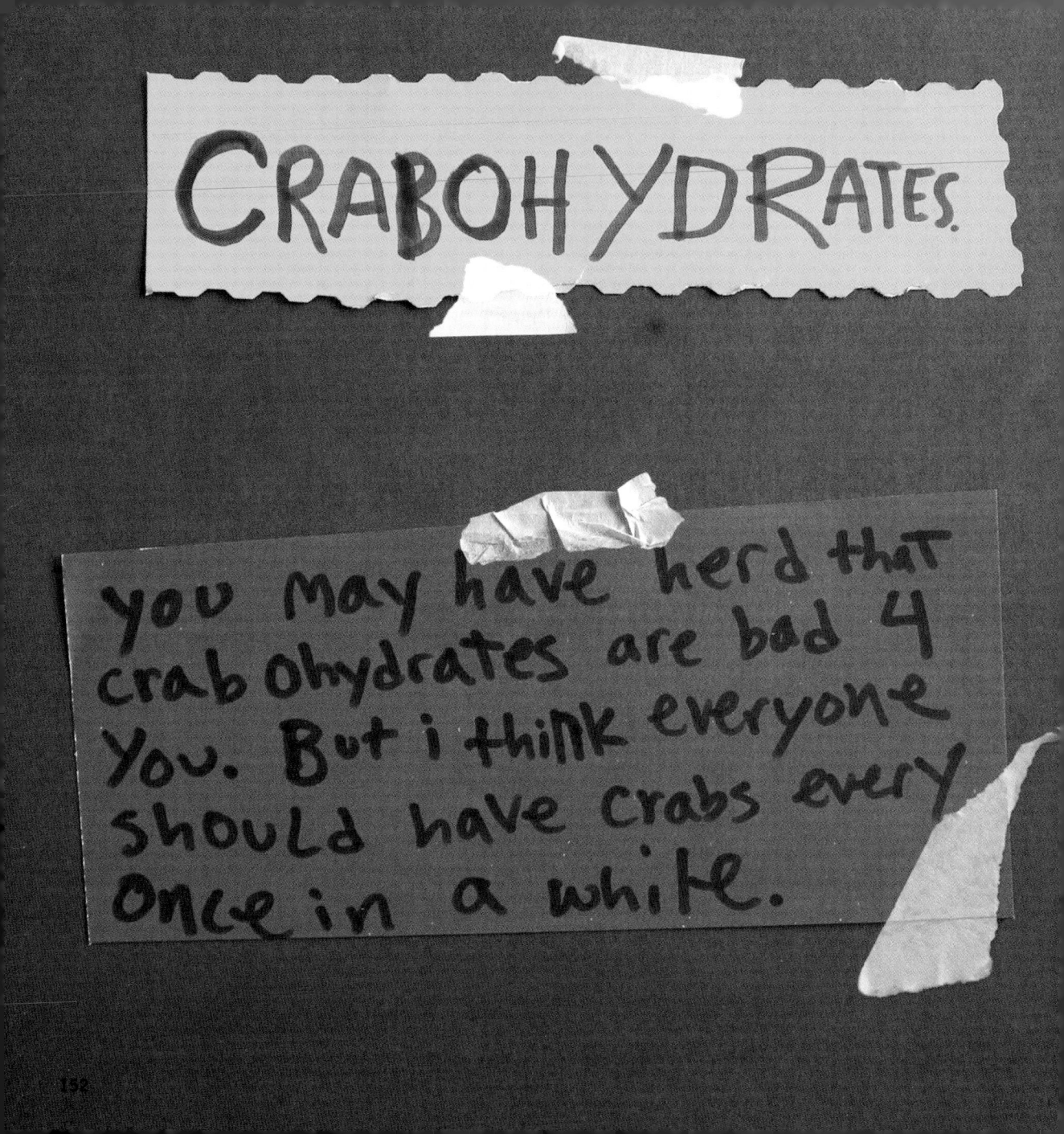
CRABOHYDRATES.
you may have herd that
crabohydrates are bad 4
you. But i think everyone
should have crabs every
once in a while.

Crabs are sneaky and can look like lots of types of food. They can be...

SOFT

CRUNCHY

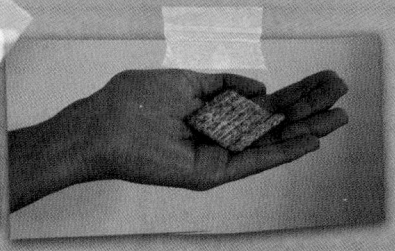

ICHY

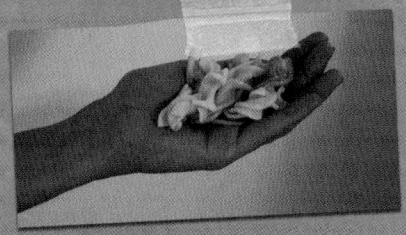

SQUINCHY

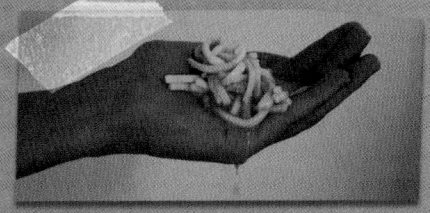

WET.

in my opinion, the more crabs you get, the better. But if your concerned about having less carbs, you can share.

HYGENE
its important to stay
clean so you dont have
get germs. Have some
one wash you once
a week

WiPiNG

"SAVE the earth By trapping the poo."

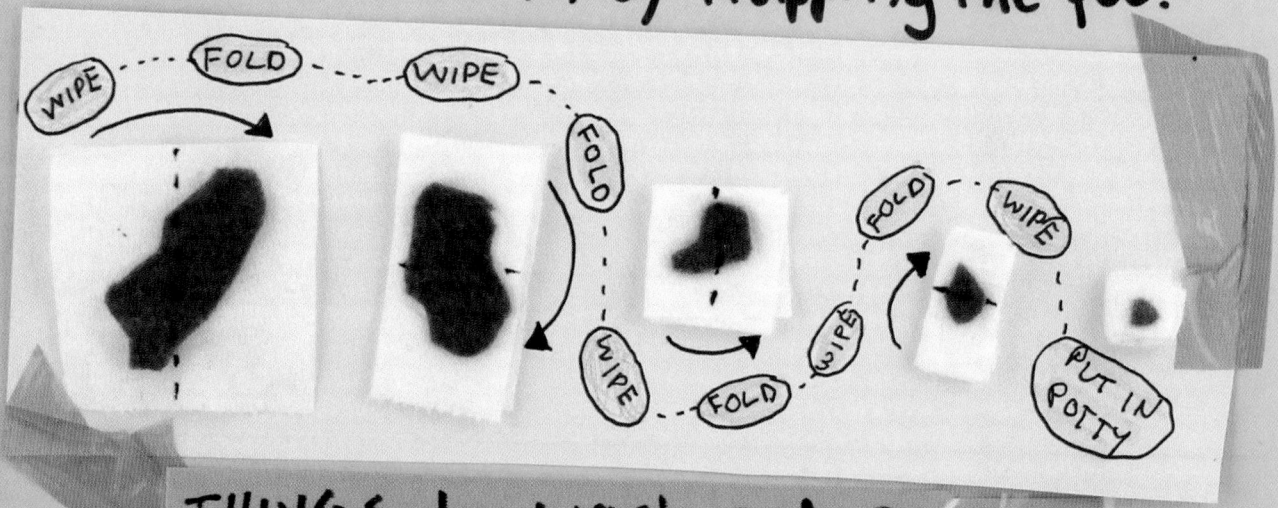

THINGS to wach out For

THE SMEAR
when it spreads instead OF coming OFF. very dangerous

THE ROLL
when the Poo rolls into Little worm Shapes.

THE TEAR
when the toilet Paper rips and your fingers poke thru.

THESUPRISE
when you think your done, But then you wipe and realize ur NOT.

THE BLOOD
When there is BLOOd.

How To Bath
Make Bubbles
get in all the creases
dont get hair wet
use toys
Save water by changing water 1 a month
Dont worry about pee water. wont change color like at the pool

How to Bath without a Bath
Hear are some ways to clean yourself w/o cleaning yourself
• Kleenex
• spit
• change clothes
• perfume
• use carsmelly dangle things
• roll in fresh cut lawn
• wipe
• run thru sprinklers
• stick your head in front of fan. Let the dirt Blow off

DOCTORS
Doctors R mean, grumpy men who just want to give you drugs and poke you.
You will sit on yucky paper for hours!!!
i will make sure my hands are wet and cold
i will poke you
My stethiscope will always be COLD...
im going to squeeze your arm so hard

How to Be your Own Doctor.

MAKE DRUGS AT HOME!

Tic Tacs look like pills.

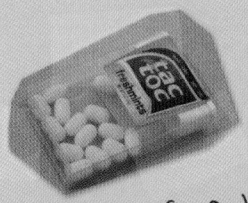

spoonfull of pudding or soup is kind of like cough syrup.

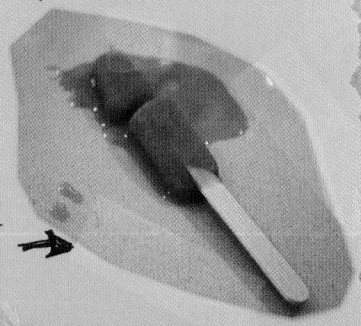

Popsicle Stick →

How to Fix a Sickness

COLD → Blanket

Broken arm → Tape cast

runny Nose → Tampons

Throwing up → Stay outside

stepped on Lego → No Hope

headache → Band aid

Something stuck in you → Get help from uncle

Puberty
CAUTION CAUTION
iF you are under the age 21 Please Skip the next 3 pages. They R inapropriate 4 you

PUBERTY

PUBerty is a time where you get hairs and smells.

You also mite experience getting chesticle lumps. cover these. ALSO you mite LEAK things. it WILL ruin Panties.

MONTHLY LADY TIME

As a girl you sometimes get leaky after puberty and you have to clean it or you could get an infetchon or ruin panties. You can make a diaper with toilet paper or use a pad. Do NOT use tampons. They are 4 sinners. That is a exit only place!

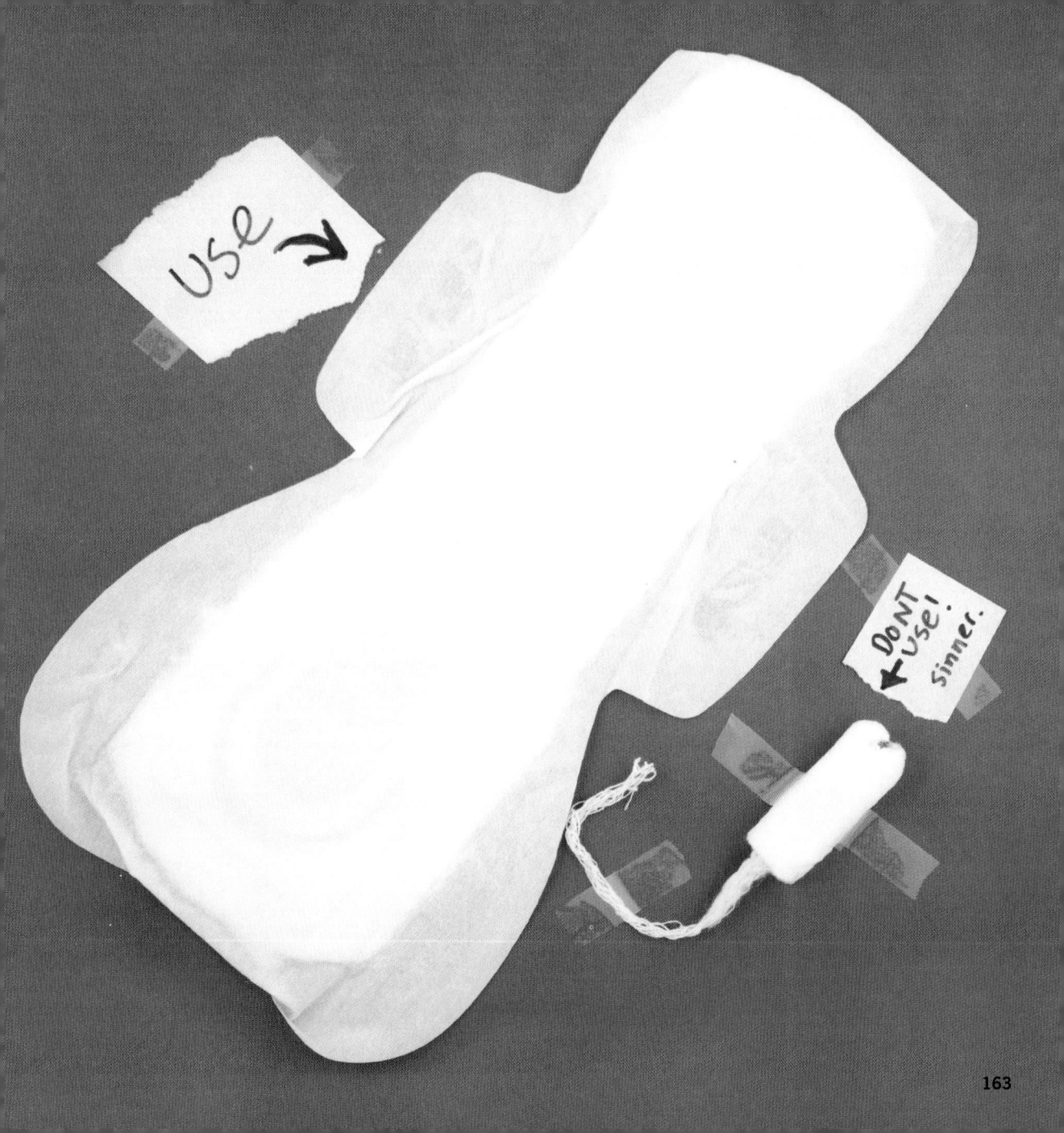
Use
DoNT
Use!
Sinner.

SLEEP
Sleep is good Because when you sleep you are getting sleep and that is good. Also when you sleep you get to dream about all the things. Hear is a dream Decoder so you No what your dreams mean.
DREAM DECODER
FLYING = you are gassy
FALLING = you are clumsy
DROWNING = you are thirsty
BOYS = you have wet the Bed
OPENING PRESENTS = DONt wake up. you will Be very upset.

Good sleep is good. Try these good sleep positions to sleep good.

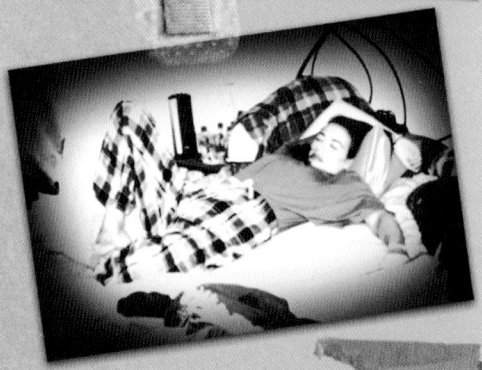

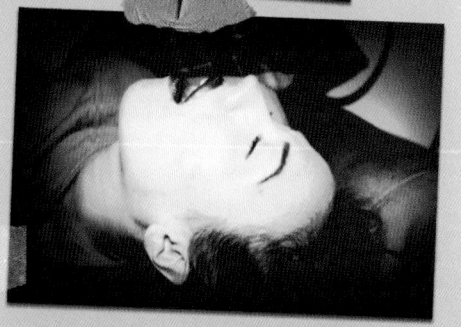

Pitchurs my uncle took to show how i sleep.

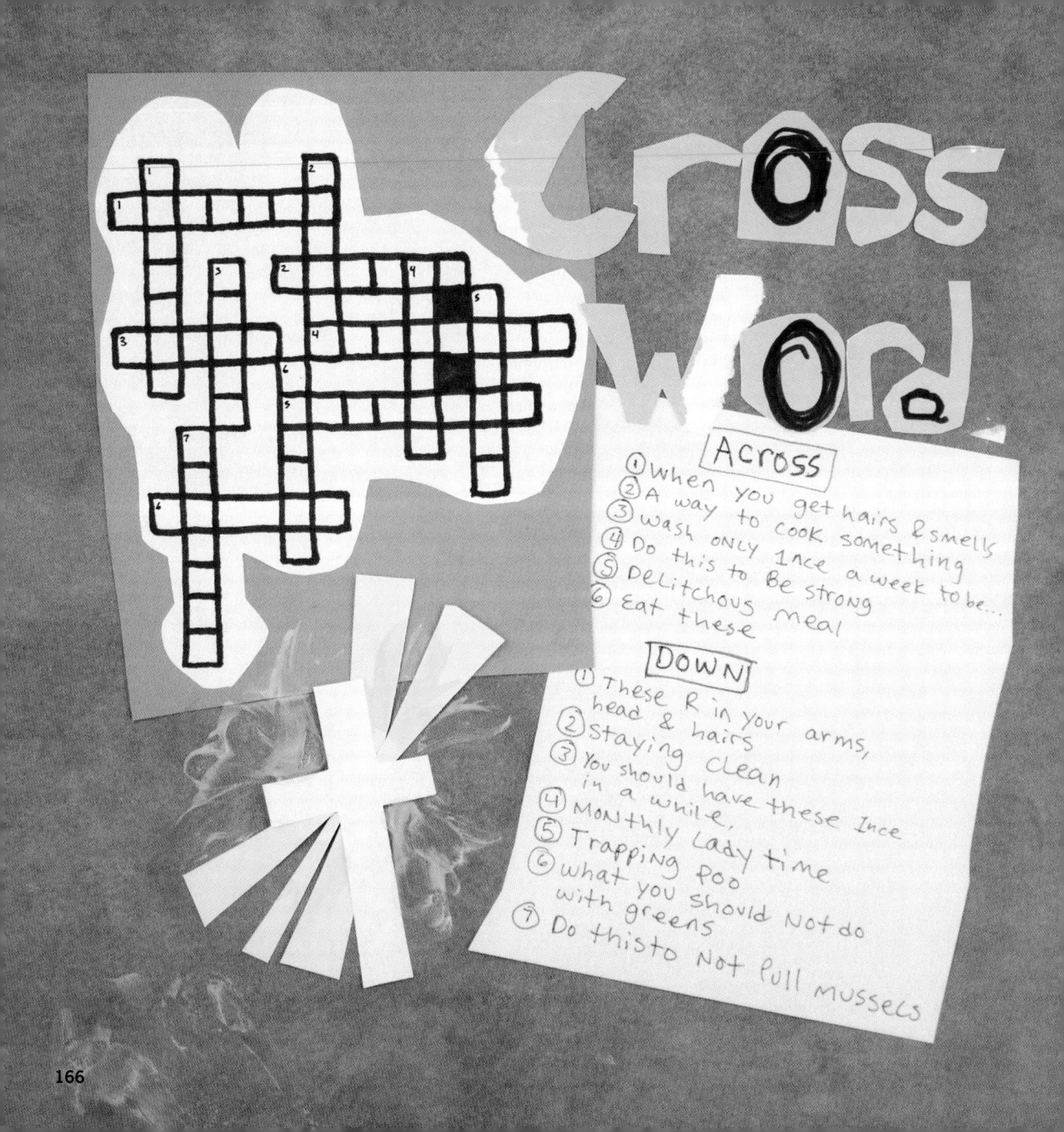
Cross Word
Across
① When you get hairs & smells
② A way to cook something
③ wash only 1nce a week to be...
④ Do this to be strong
⑤ Delitchous meal
⑥ Eat these
DOWN
① These R in your arms, head & hairs
② Staying clean
③ You should have these 1nce in a while,
④ Monthly lady time
⑤ Trapping poo
⑥ what you should not do with greens
⑦ Do this to not pull mussels

SelfEsteem

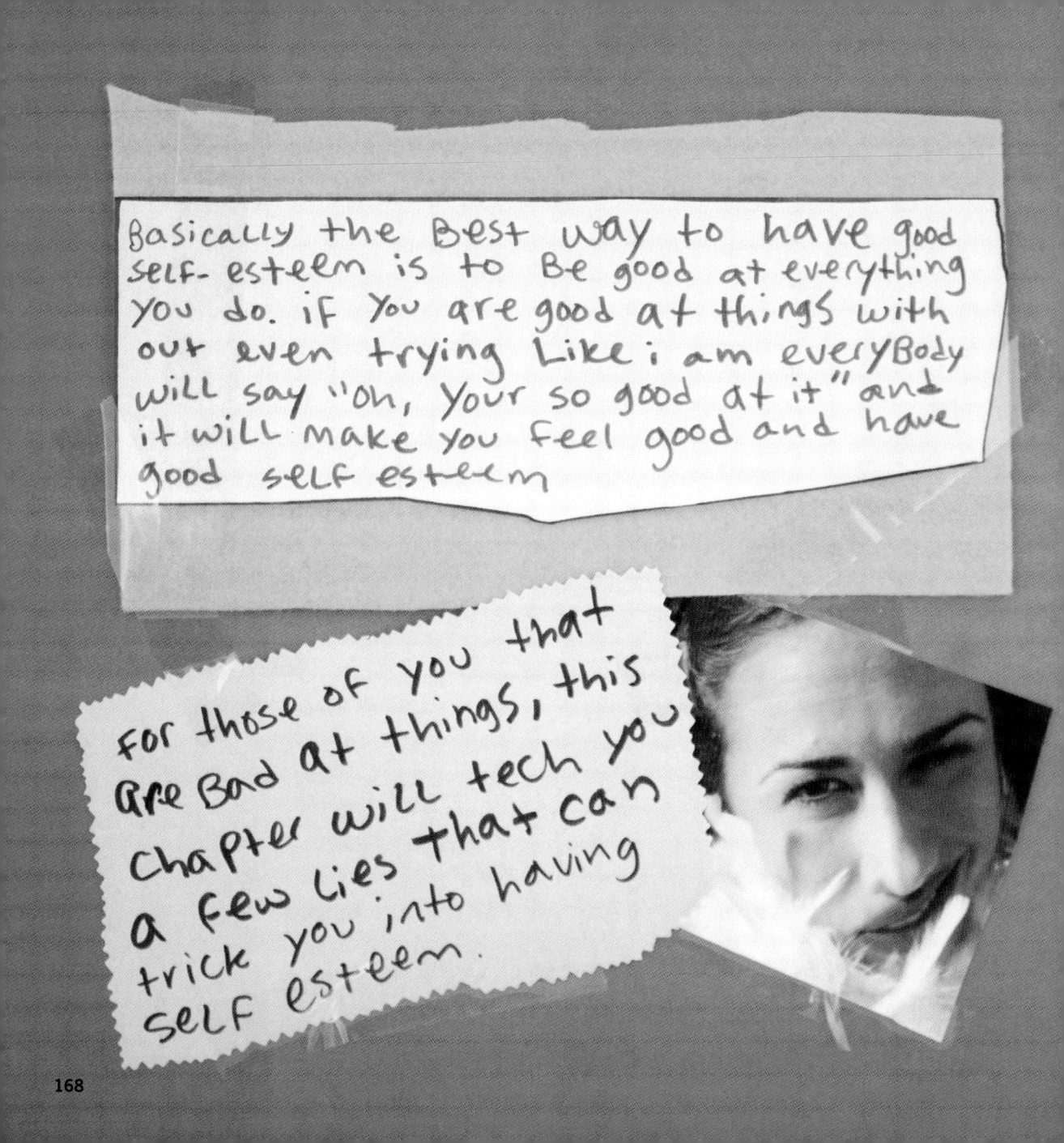

Basically the Best way to have good self-esteem is to Be good at everything you do. if you are good at things with out even trying Like i am everyBody will say "oh, your so good at it" and it will make you feel good and have good self esteem

For those of you that Are Bad at things, this chapter will tech you a few lies that can trick you into having self esteem.

Mirror Exercises

Look into the mirror and say these types of things.

you ARE BOOTiful.

Look how smart you are

i am a celebrity

if you are ugly, skip to the next page.

Positive Thoughts
Tell yourself these things
Everything that is meant to be will happen... unless i dont like it.
im perfect the way i am so you should change
if you dream it, you can do it! But if you have a naked dream dont do that you will get in trouble
I slept in this morning
i can stick my whole fist in my mouth.
your not the boss of me.
im hotter than everyone and i love cheese.

PUT DOWN OTHERS
A great way to make yourself feel better is to make other people feel worse.
YOU
Feeling Better
PUT DOWNS
DISSES
INSULTS
OTHER PERSON
DIAGRAM

Hear are some good insult ideas.
Nice Face... NOT!
i dont Like you.
you arent even that pretty
you wish you looked like me.

More insults
i know you are but what am i?
NO.
YOUR MOM!
you look really good... ON OPPOSITE DAY!

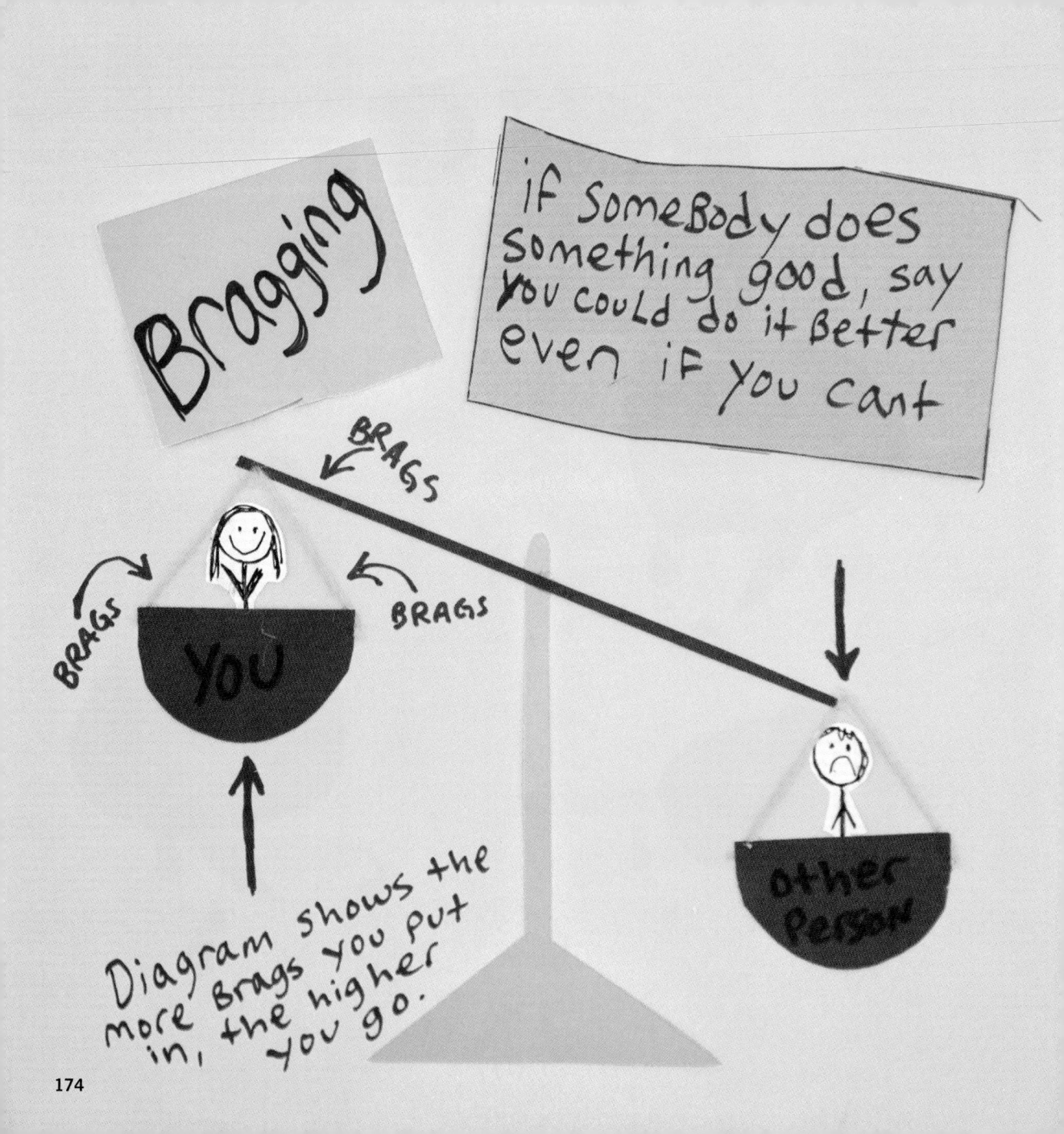
Bragging
if SomeBody does something good, say you could do it Better even if you cant
BRAGS
BRAGS
BRAGS
YOU
other Person
Diagram shows the more Brags you put in, the higher you go.

2 Types of Bragging

① Talk about your talents:
Talk about something you can do and say that you can do it the Best.

② Brag over other peoples Brags:
interrupt someone who is Bragging and Brag Louder and Better then them.

Games R a gr8 way to [redacted] higher self esteem. So play By yourself so you always win

staring contest

thumb war

Tag
Tug o' war
rock, paper scissors

BODY LANGUAGE
BAD
VS.
GOOD
Smiling too much seems like your hiding something
VS.
Just Look Natural
Bad Sitting teckneek Looks weak and Closed off
VS.
more available Posture
Handshake is too touchy
VS.
Less germs.

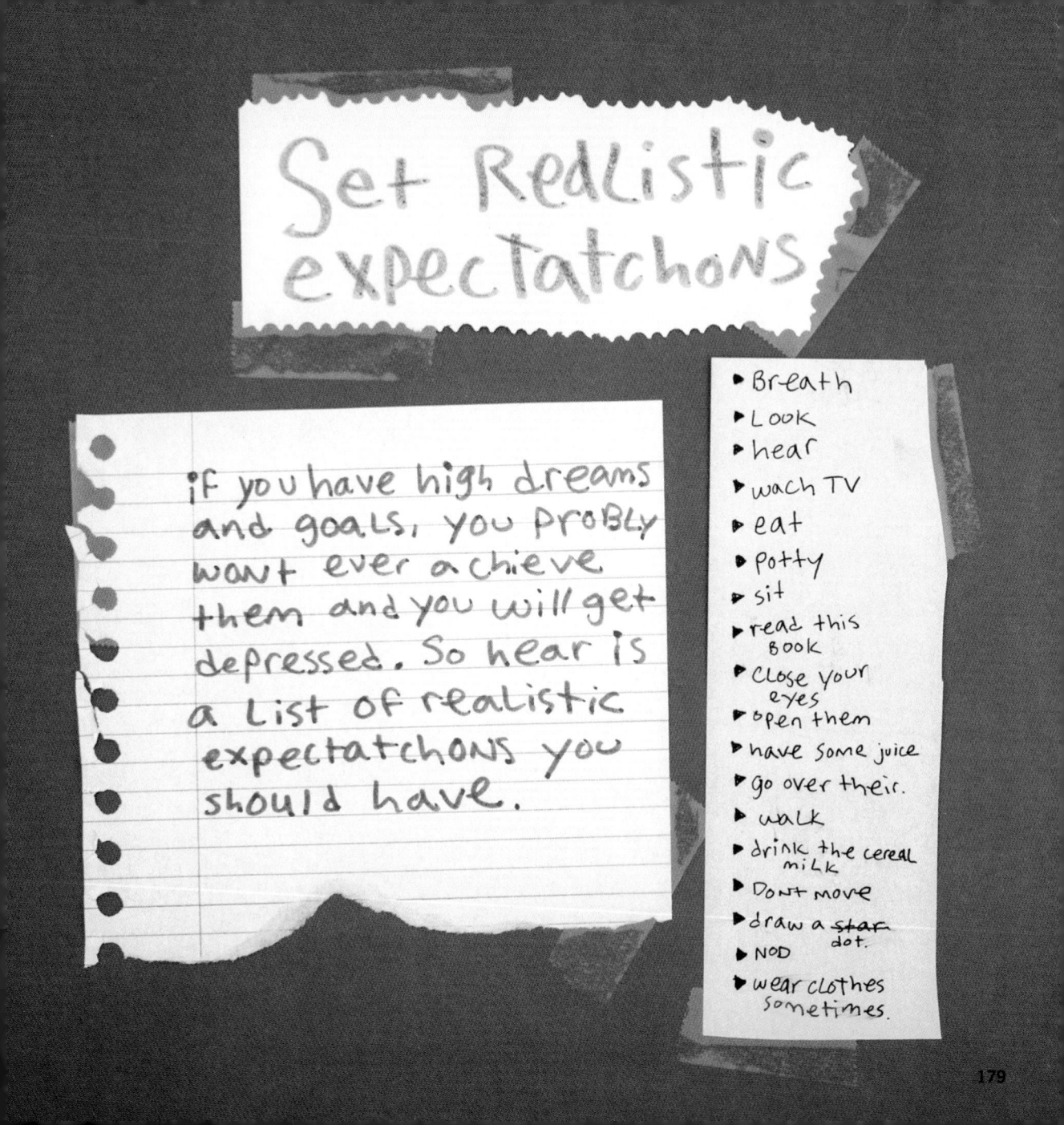

Set Redlistic expectatchons

if you have high dreams and goals, you probly wont ever achieve them and you will get depressed. So hear is a List of realistic expectatchons you should have.

- Breath
- Look
- hear
- wach TV
- eat
- potty
- sit
- read this Book
- Close your eyes
- open them
- have some juice
- go over their.
- walk
- drink the cereal milk
- Dont move
- draw a ~~star~~ dot.
- NOD
- wear clothes sometimes.

Secret code to having a happy life. crack the code to find out what it is.
H M E A C I N D W T S V O R

Color by Number
1 red
2 blue
3 pink
4 brown
5 purple
6 yellow
7 black
1=RED 2=BLUE 3=PINK 4=BROWN 5=PURPLE
6=YELLOW 7=BLACK

if your self esteem
is still really low you
can cut out this mask
and people will com-
pliment you and
tell you how pritty
you R so you will
get confident.

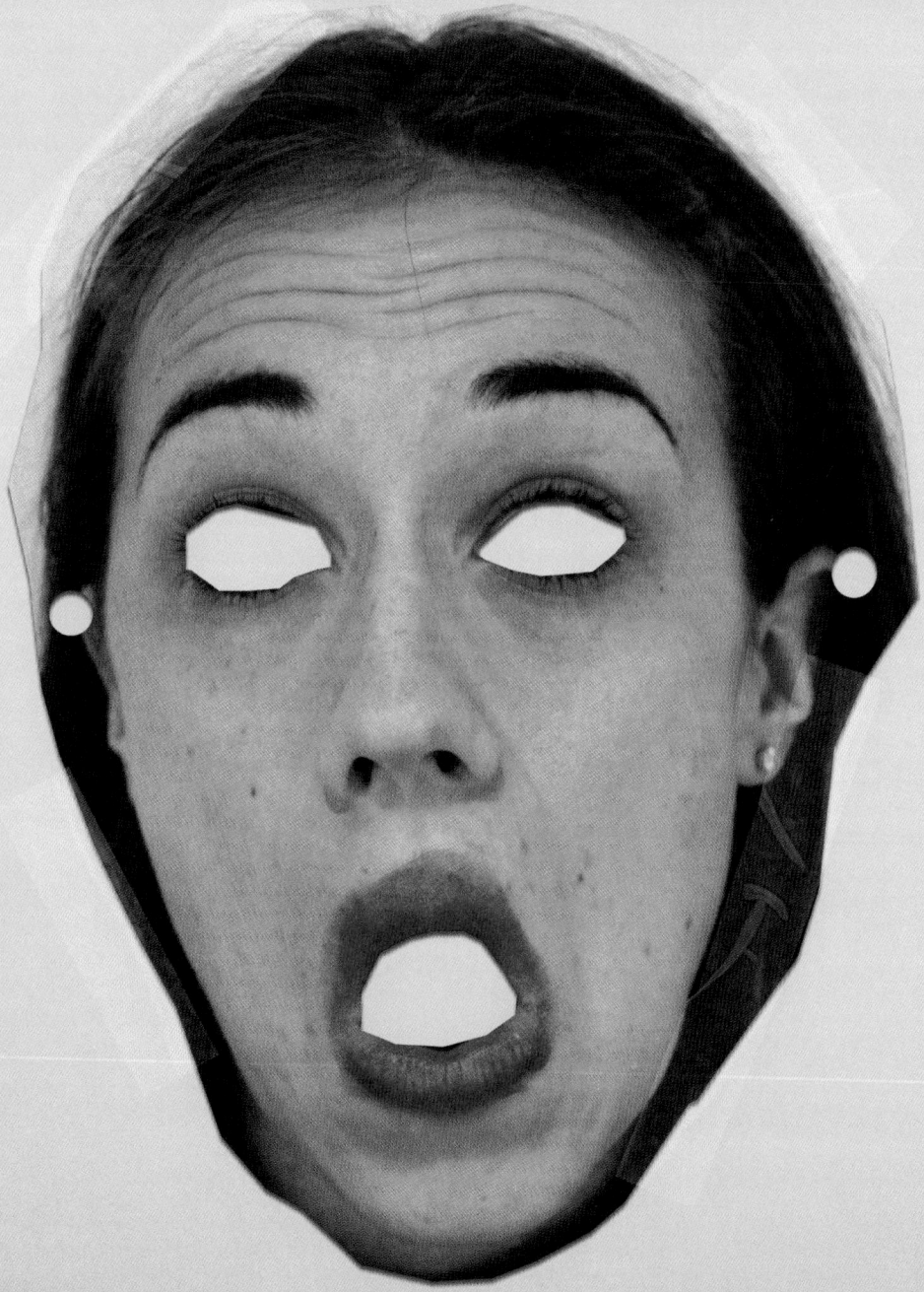

Do something Nice 4 yourself.
eat all the frosting off cupcakes
make someone do something nice 4 you
take mom's money
patting yourself
icy drink baths
take an insects wings
do a little dance
sing yourself a song
pop bubble wrap
not sharing
pick that scab
break every single crayon in someone elses box and then put them back.
suck all the salt off the peanuts
Eat extra meat

Self Esteem Word Scramble
FLTAHNUK
AYPHP
AiVEERCT
OVLGiN
PiGNiUVG
MREDA
VStiiEPO
Final Word:

How To Do
Children

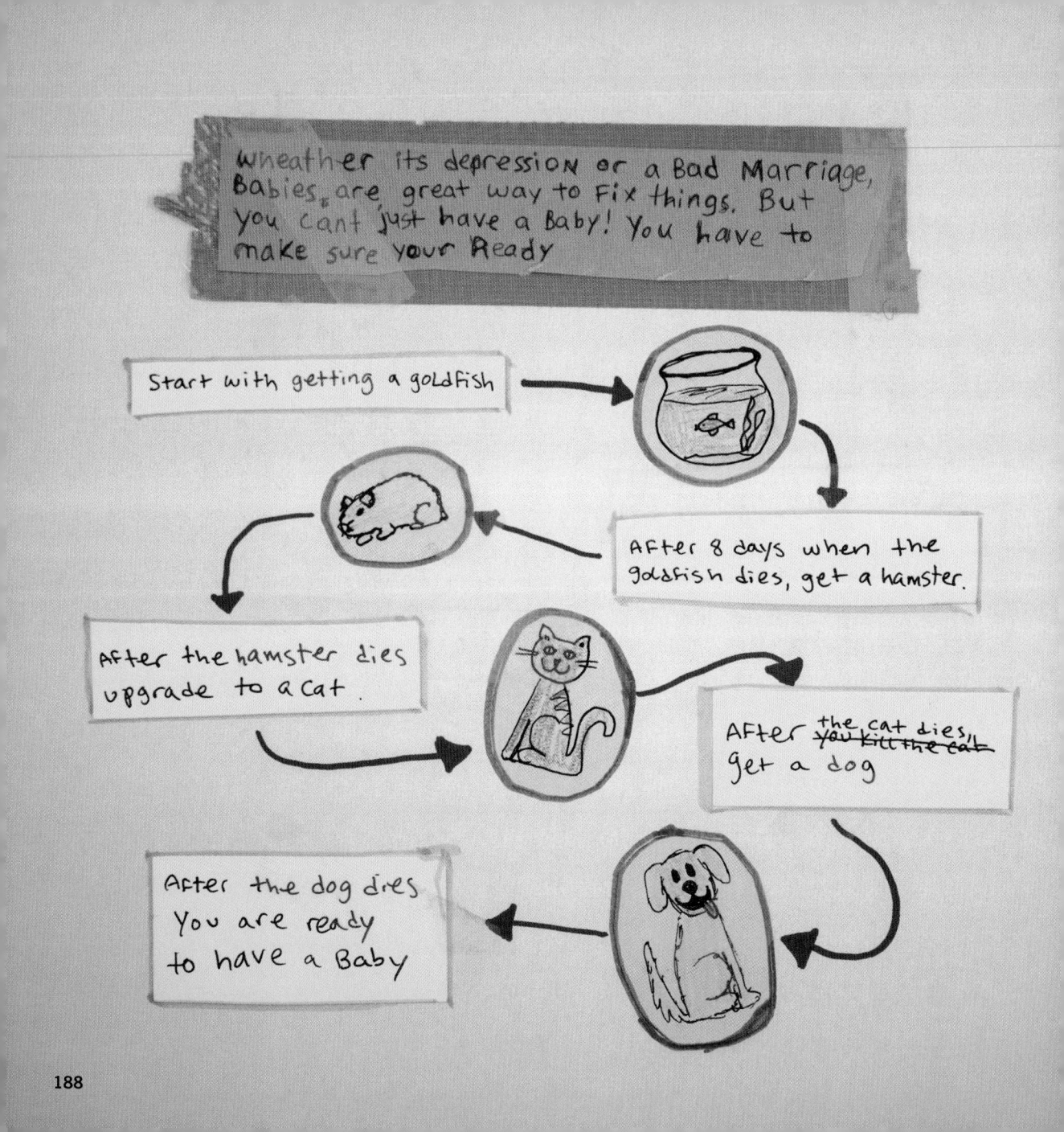
wheather its depression or a Bad Marriage, Babies are great way to Fix things. But you Cant just have a Baby! You have to make sure your Ready
Start with getting a goldfish
After 8 days when the goldfish dies, get a hamster.
After the hamster dies upgrade to a Cat.
After the cat dies, ~~you kill the cat~~ get a dog
After the dog dies You are ready to have a Baby

Another good way to get ready is to practice. this is called...

BABY SITTING

Babysitting is great Because if you decide you dont like it you can just leave

BABYSITTING TIPS
PROBLEMS
FIXES
CRYING BABY
Baby getting too close
hiccups
Loud Baby
escaping Baby
Baby eats something he shoulant
ANNOYING BABY
GIVE IT WATER upside down
Leave
Ear Plugs
Put something in his mouth
Preted you didnt see
Push away
tie it to something

Diaper Changing

i Dont Like using regular Diapers Because they smell too much Like Babies. A good Alternative is a towel.

STEP 1

PUT A TOWEL UNDER THE BABY'S TOOKIE.

STEP 2

PUT A WIPE IN THERE SO YOU CLEAN LESS LATER.

STEP 3

FOLD the diaper up and over the Baby

STEP 4

TIE it all together with a rope.

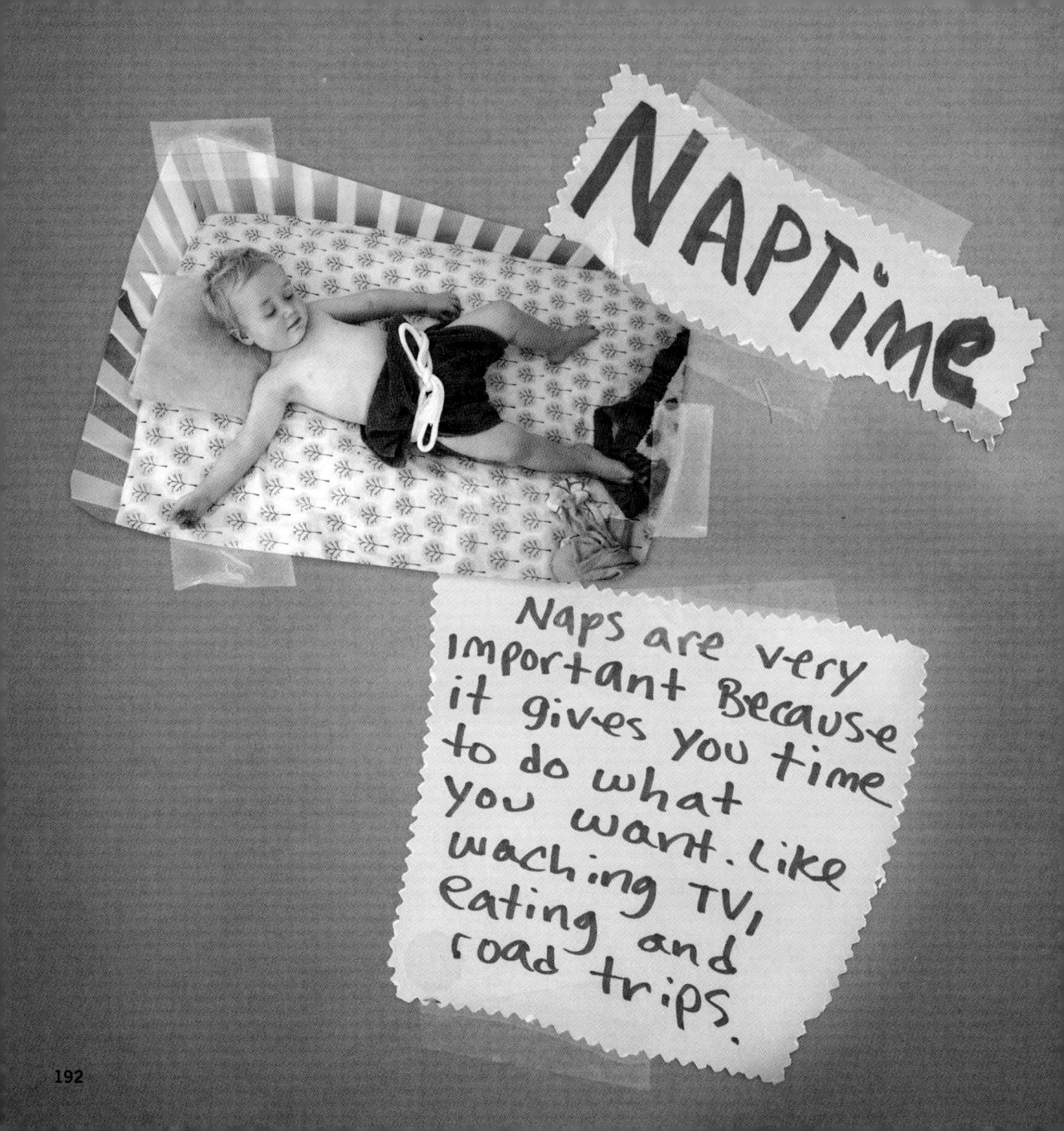
NAPTime
Naps are very
important Because
it gives you time
to do what
you want. Like
wacking TV,
eating and
road trips.

Hear are some good positchens to Hold your Baby with

No Hands

the Backpack

it Pooped

crusifiction

As you have read, Babies are useless until they get older. Eventually they will Become toddlers or i like to call them: SLAVES. This is the time when you can have them do things For you.

Things a toddler can Do 4 you...
Foot massage
clean
kill spiders
fan you
eat crust

Fun Activities

Sometimes you have to Do things with Kids. These Few activities can Be Fun For you and ur children

HIDE AND SEAK

have your kid hide and then do something esise while they are distracted

PLAYING DRESS UP

you can have them dress as a dog or a homeless

Play Horsey

Looks fun right?

PAPER DOLL

here you have you're
very own papre doll.
dress her up in
different outfits for
different ocajons.

How To Play at The Playground

Tiny hands are good for sand picking

Kids cant push you high enough to get scared

Kids can catch you on the slide

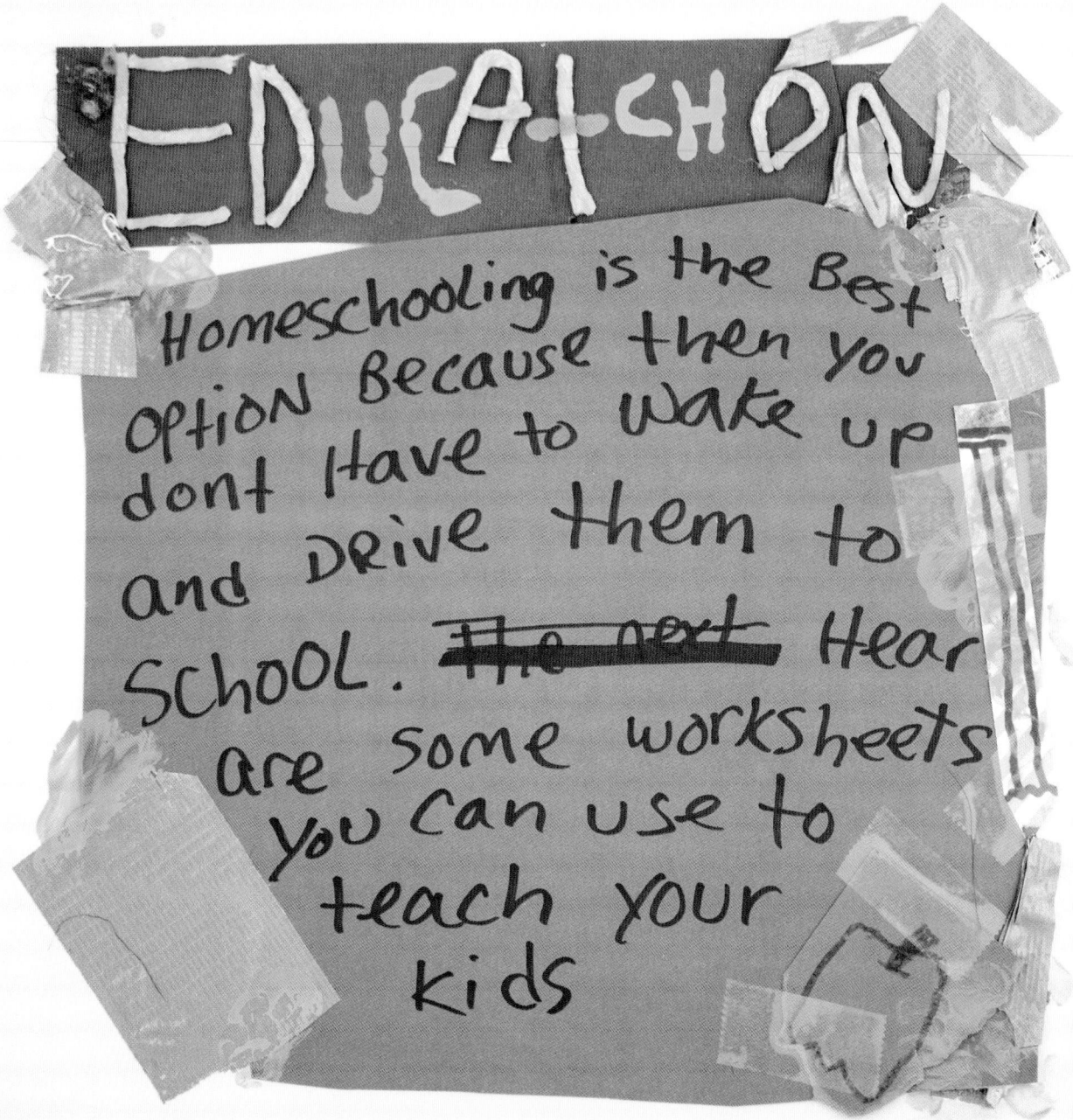
EDUCATION
Homeschooling is the Best
option Because then you
dont Have to wake up
and Drive them to
School. ~~The next~~ Hear
are some worksheets
you can use to
teach your
kids

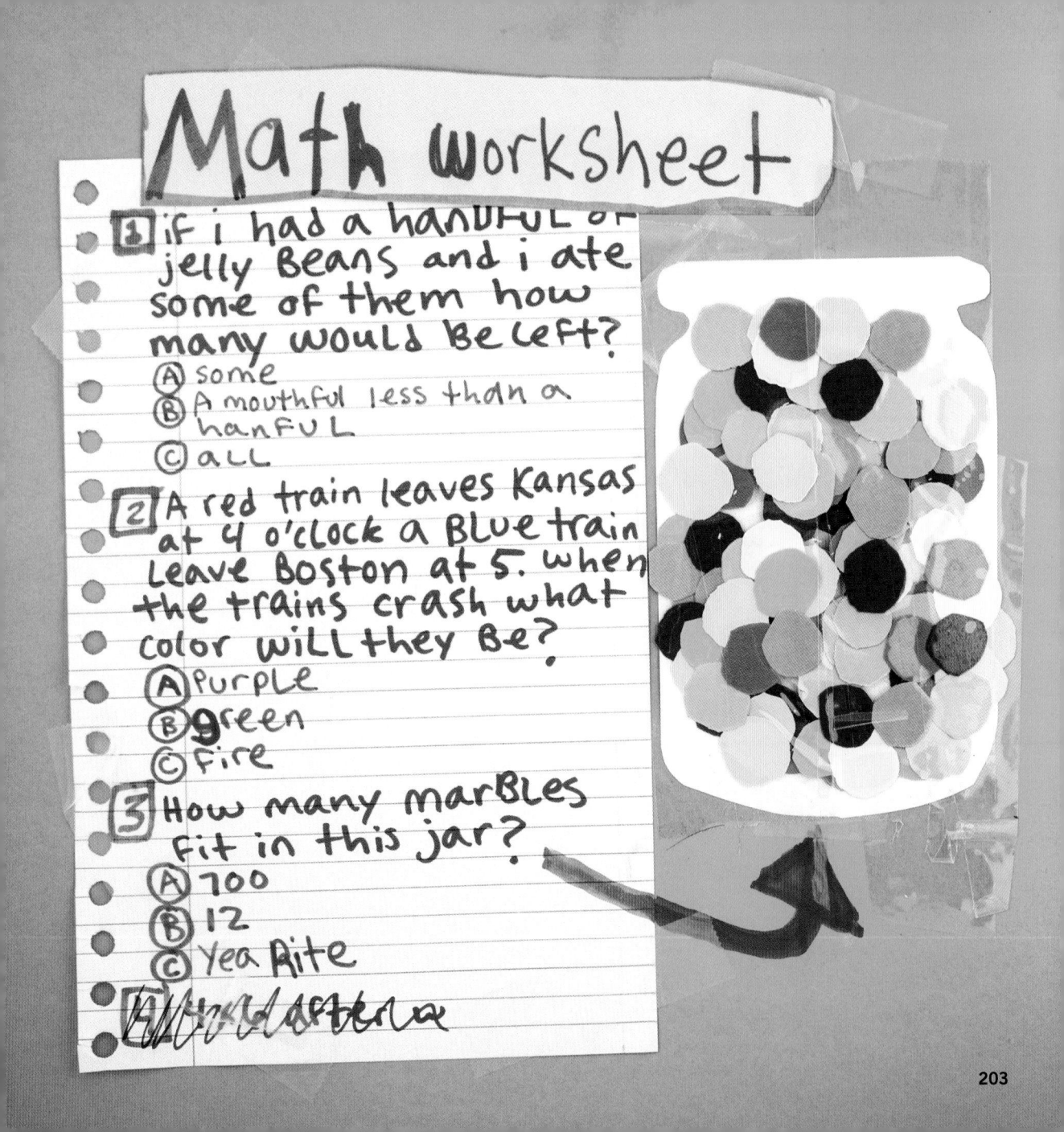
Math worksheet
1 if i had a handful of jelly Beans and i ate some of them how many would Be left?
A some
B A mouthful less than a hanful
C all
2 A red train leaves Kansas at 4 o'clock a Blue train Leave Boston at 5. when the trains crash what color will they Be?
A purple
B green
C fire
3 How many marBles fit in this jar?
A 700
B 12
C Yea Rite

ENGLish Worksheet
Fill in the Blanks
1 Hair is to crunchy AS _____ is to soft
A Hands B Peas C Loshen
2 Tickles are to UNCLE AS _____ is to Bae
A slaps B kisses C strokes
3 Spitcy is to Pepper AS _____ is to scratchy
A Tags B grass C Hair snow
4 Flaky is to SQUishy AS Pretty is to _____
A ugly B smart C BoTh
5 Hairs are to Fingers AS _____ are to eye crusties
A toes B sticks C Rags

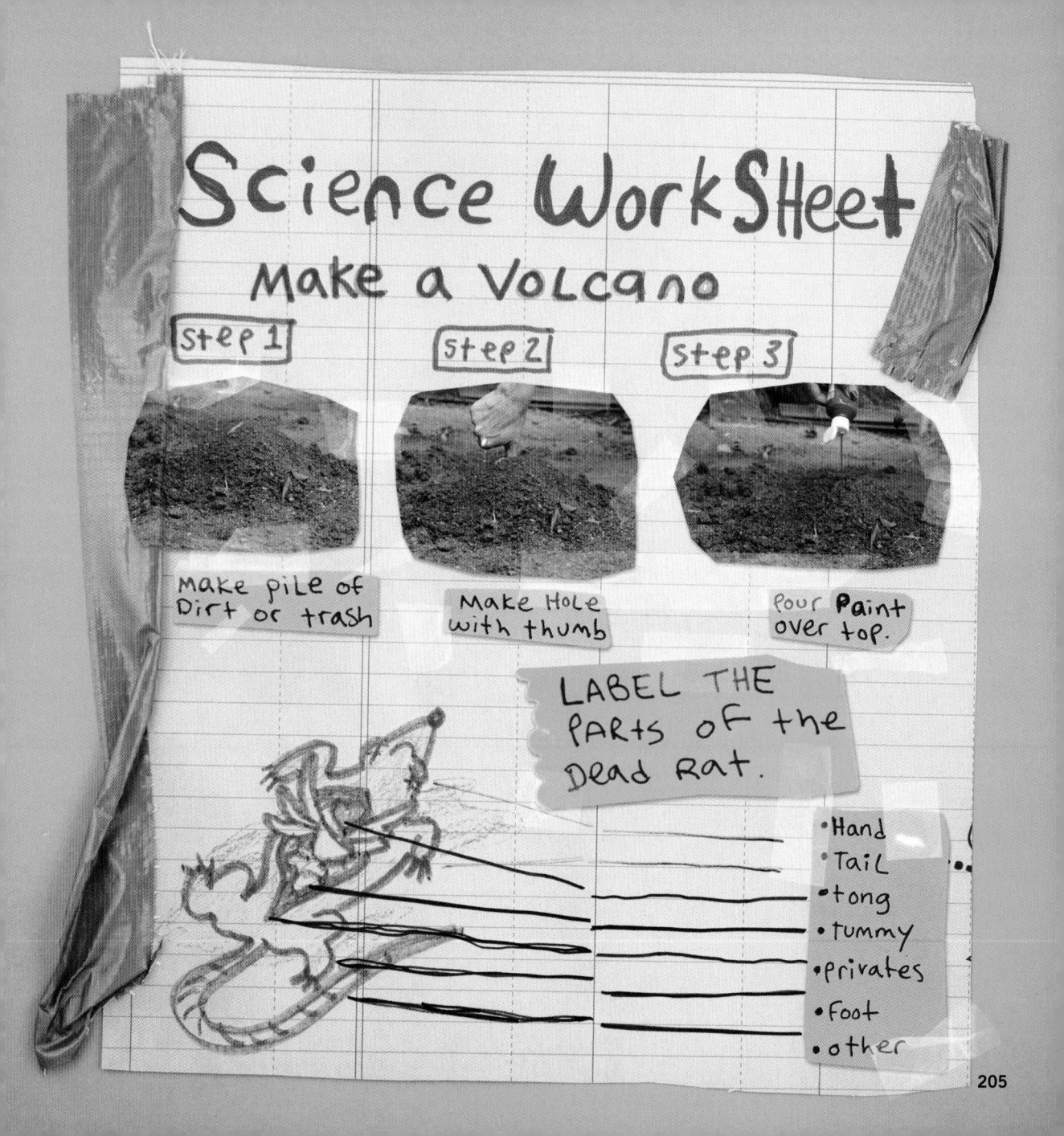
Science WorkSheet
Make a Volcano
Step 1
Step 2
Step 3
Make pile of Dirt or trash
Make Hole with thumb
Pour Paint over top.
LABEL THE PARTS OF the Dead Rat.
•Hand
•Tail
•tong
•tummy
•privates
•Foot
•other

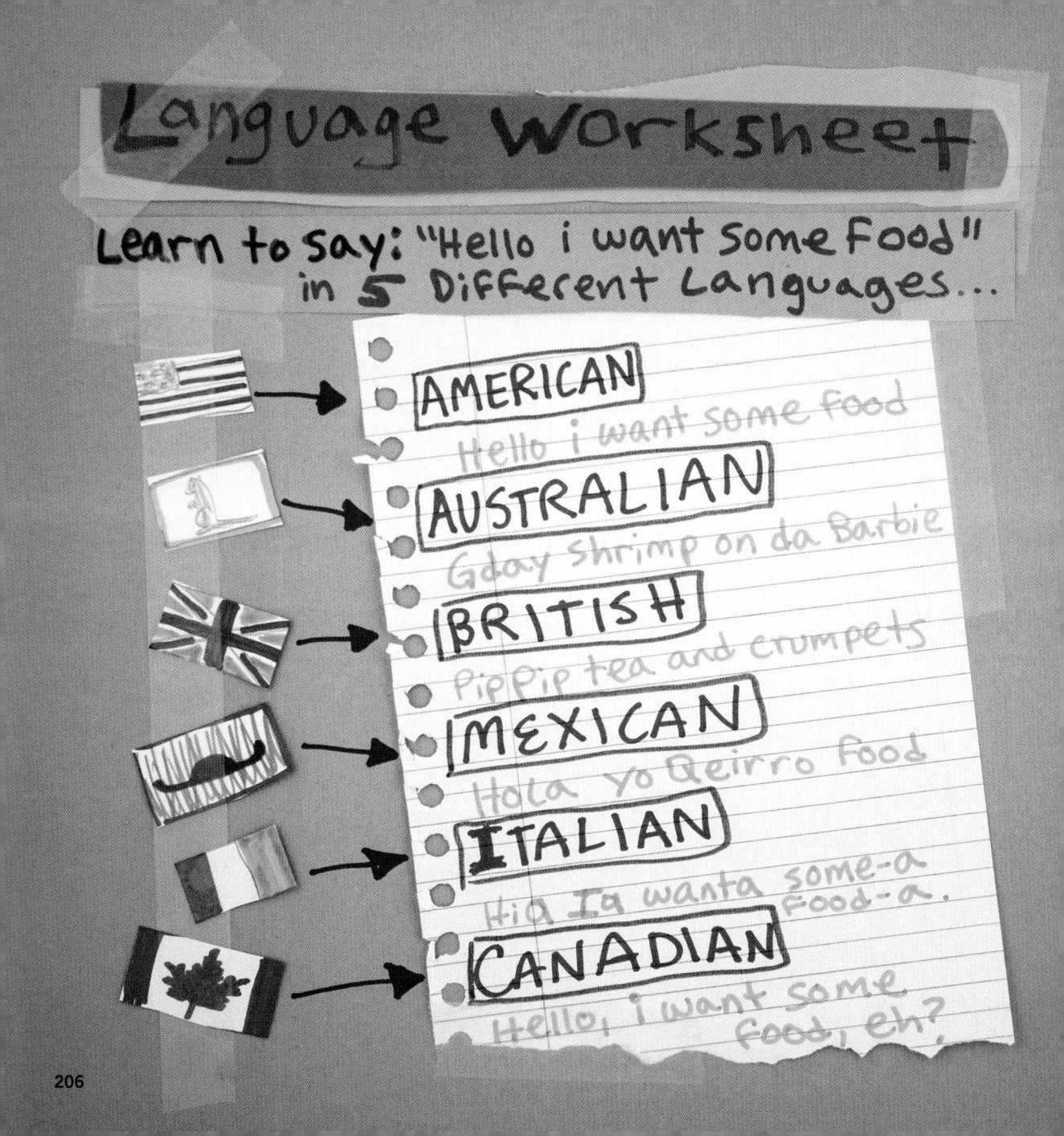
Language Worksheet
Learn to say: "Hello i want some Food"
in 5 Different Languages...
AMERICAN
Hello i want some food
AUSTRALIAN
Gday shrimp on da Barbie
BRITISH
Pippip tea and crumpets
MEXICAN
Hola yo Qeirro food
ITALIAN
Hia Ia wanta some-a food-a.
CANADIAN
Hello, i want some food, eh?

HISTORY

History Started when Christopher Columbus Discovered America then he had Thanksgiving with

the indians. that was the 1st supper. then there was CowBoys. then astronats. then i was Born. Questions

who started history?
what was thankgiving called?
who came Before Astronats?
who ended History?

Coloring Page

LIFE
Hacks

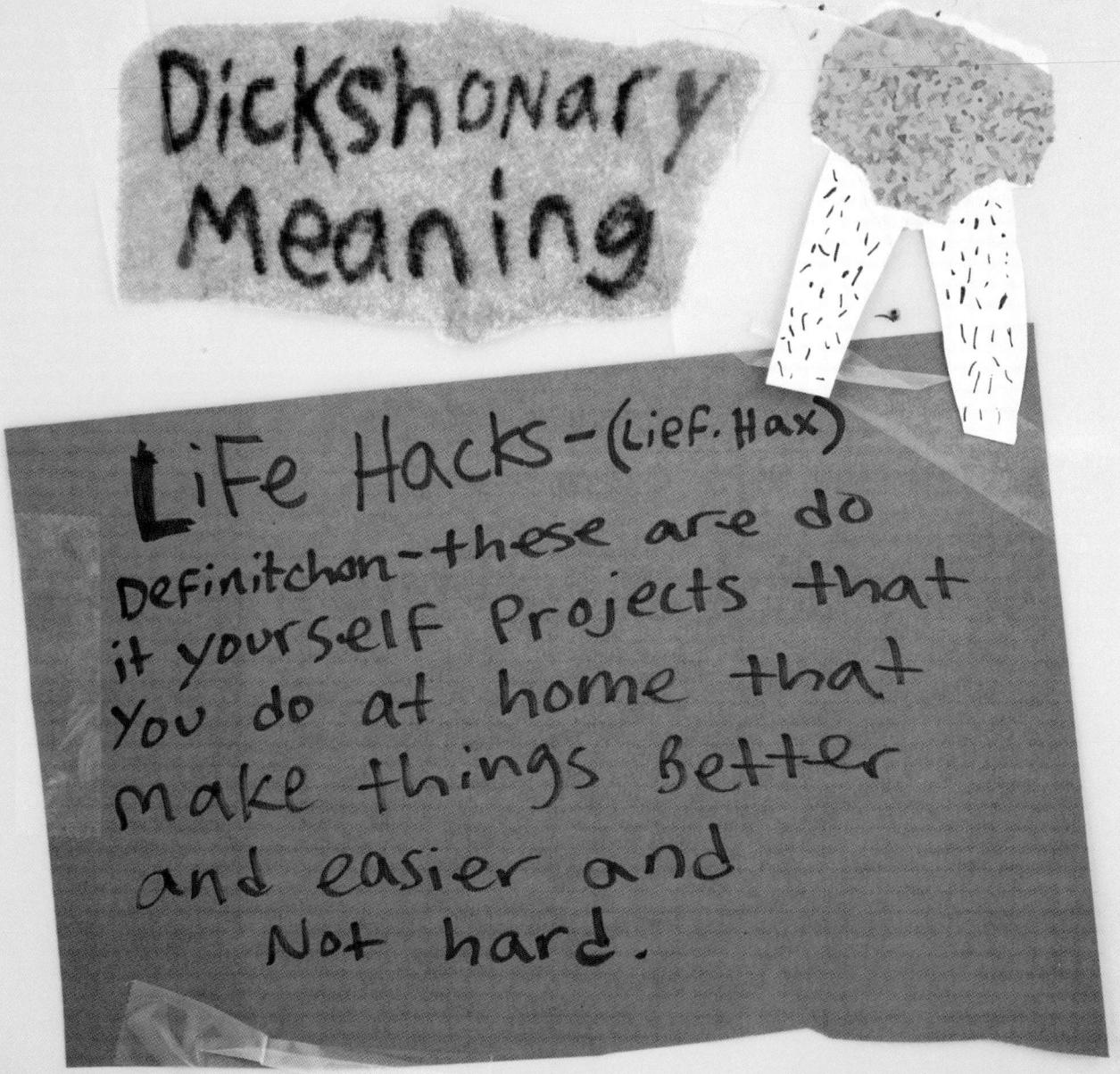
Dickshonary
Meaning
Life Hacks-(Lief. Hax)
Definitchon-these are do
it yourself Projects that
you do at home that
make things better
and easier and
Not hard.

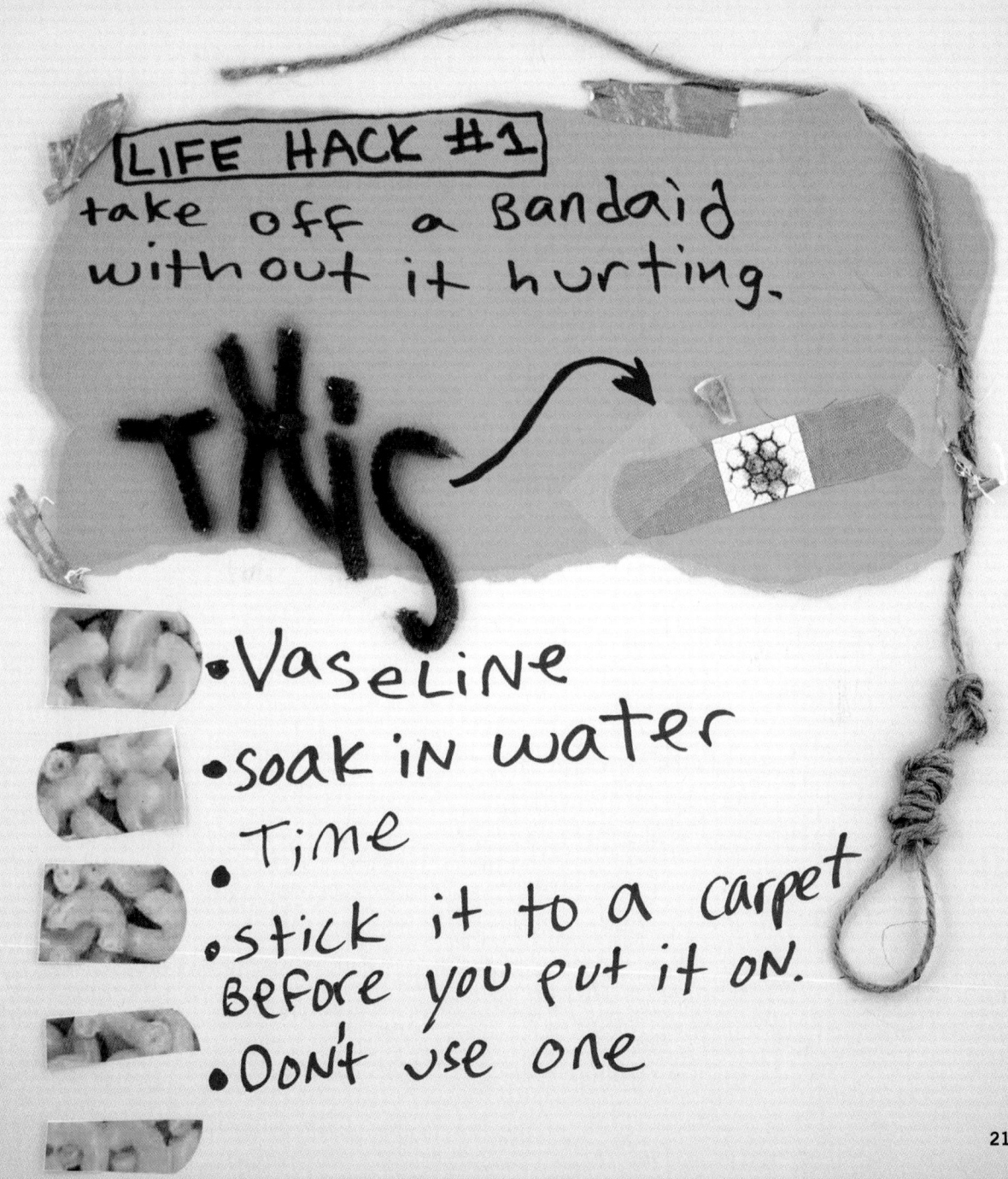
LIFE HACK #1
take off a Bandaid without it hurting.
THIS
•Vaseline
•soak in water
•Time
•stick it to a carpet before you put it on.
•Don't use one

Life Hacks #2
Get gum out of Hair.
This
Also this
Eat it
Cut it
Pick it
Shape it like a bow
color it the same as your hair
Put more hair over it.

Life Hacks #3
How To Make Homemade Shampoo
1 Find a Bottle to put it in.
2 use Lipgloss to keep hair moist
3 squirt in hand sanitizer to keep hair clean
4 Pour in some juice to make it smell good
5 Put it in hair to use it.

LiFE Hack #4

3 ways to crack egg with NO shells

smash egg in BOWL

use Fingers to pick out shell pieces

smash egg in Plastic Bag

Put egg in Bag. smash. cut off corner and squirt out egg. use fingers to pick out smaller shell pieces.

smash on counter

scoop up egg with fingers and put into Bowl. Leave shells on counter.

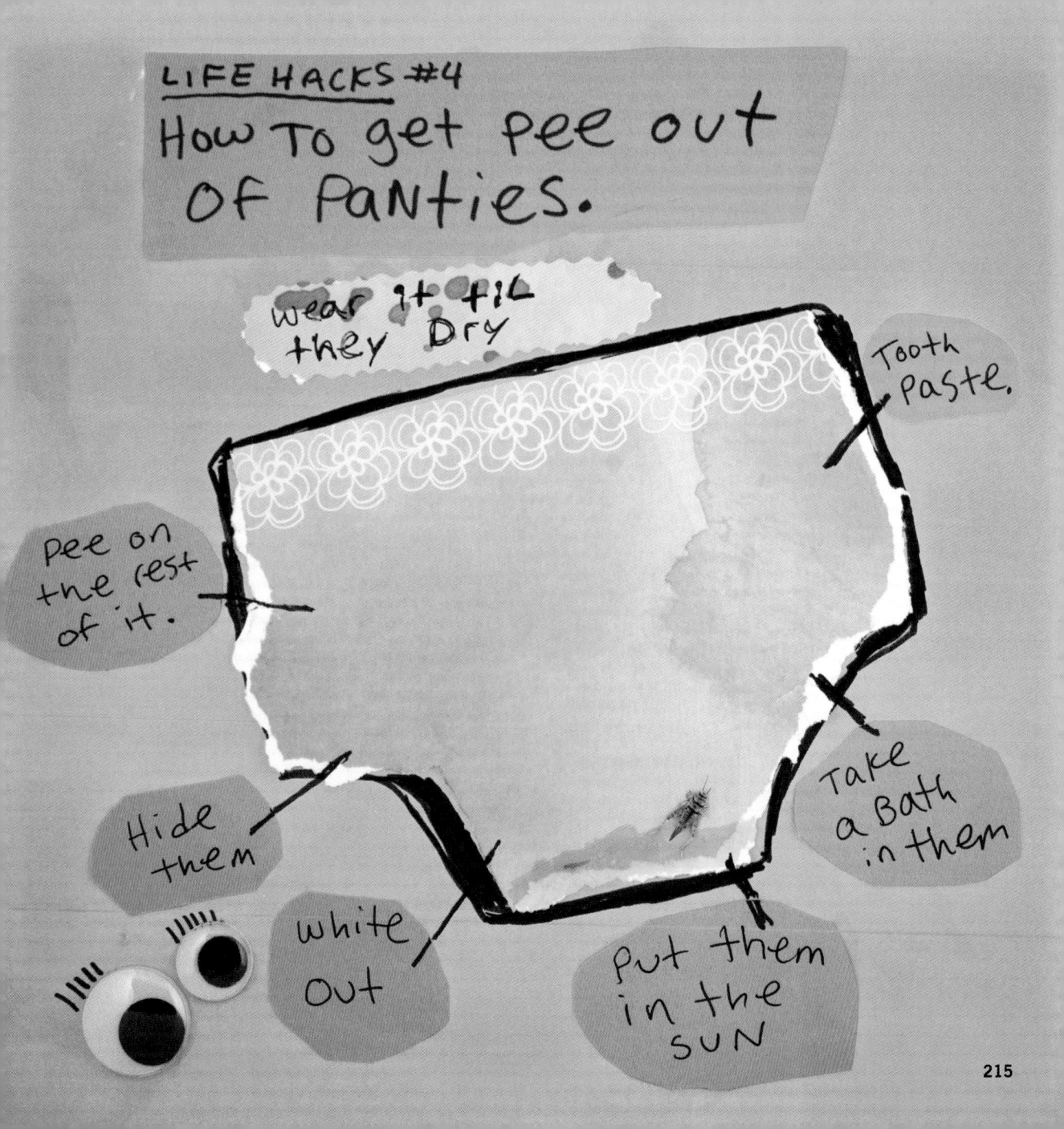
LIFE HACKS #4
How To get pee out of Panties.
wear it till they Dry
Tooth Paste.
Pee on the rest of it.
Take a Bath in them
Hide them
white Out
put them in the SUN

OPENING Things

Hear are some things that are hard to open and how to open them.

SODA CAN

cut in half with a knife.

BONUS you get two cups

Scan this with your phone to see a video tutorial.

Pickle jar

Ask your uncle to open it.

BONUS: you get to eat a pickle.

CAN OF BEANS
use a hammer.
BONUS: use BACK OF hammer as a spoon
Bag OF CHiPS
squeeze the Bag
BONUS: makes more tiny chips
MUSTard Packet
Bite it
BONUS: suprise squirts

Ways 2 lock A door w/o A lock
• Foot against the Door
• tape
• Hold it closed
• gum
• rope
• vaseline on Doornob

Other uses For Household Items
Apple Pen Holder
Q-tip match
Hair &Pencil toothBrush
Sweatshirt Pants
sock hair thing
BANDAid Tape
Toothpick Qtip
Phone watch
tissue Box shoe

How to get rid of

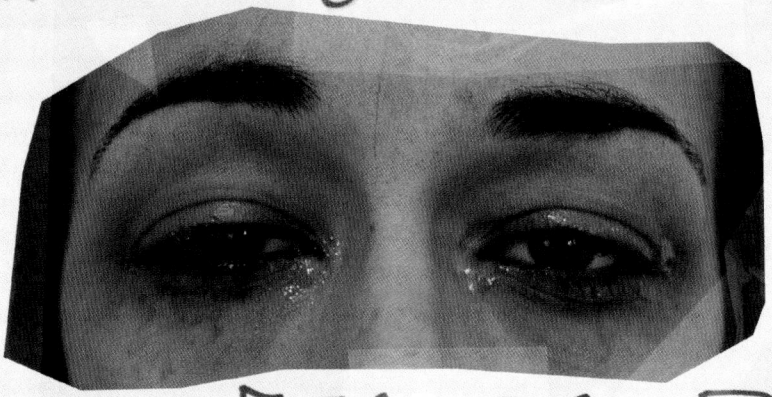

PINK EYE

STEP 1 - rub on peanut butter

STEP 2 - squeeze lemon in

STEP 3 - cover with toilet paper

STEP 4 - when it burns wipe off with piece of bread and eat it.

Get More out of your
Bathroom
Toilet top cover
Stylish Hat
Toilet Rug
Bib for eating
Hair Brush
toilet Brush
toilet paper rolls
Binoculars
Plunger
Bowl on a stick

How 2 Fix Pants with No Pockets
You will need
This & this
Staple Bags to sides of pants
Why This is Better
• place to put hands
• You can carry things
• water proof
• You can see whats inside
• Keeps Leftovers Fresh

How to make a LAMP
① roll paper into cone
② Light a candle
③ Put cone over candle

5 things you've ben doing wrong!

① Pealing a orange

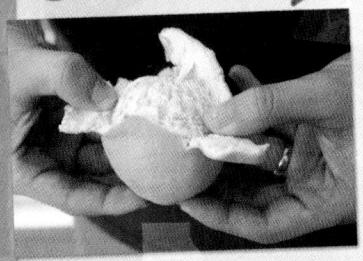

WRONG

pealing oranges is hard and spitcy under your nails. Dont Do it instead poke the orange and suck out the insides Like a yogurt pack

RITE

② tying your shoes

WRONG

tying your shoes is confusing and they come undone Just tape them instead

RITE

③ sitting ON the toilet

WRONG!

most people sit on the potty like its a chair. its not. sit on it for best squeezing leverage

RITE!

④ Eating a Burrito

WRONG!

most people start at one end and eat there way to the other side. if you start at the middle you can suck out the guts.

RITE!

⑤ untangling ear buds

WRONG!

people spend way to much time un-tangleing headfones. just cut out the tangles and tape back together

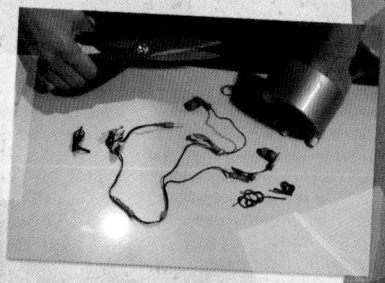

RITE!

DIY CRAFT IDEAS
Shell Frame
get a Frame and glue snails from your garden around it to make it pritty
HAir DOLLS
Twist left over or chewed up hairs into a doll shaped FUN for cuddles

SCARF
use toilet paper and Decorate with markers & stickers
PURSE
Take a paper Bag and carry it.
SNOW GLOBE
Tape a pitchur into a jar and put Little white things in it Like paper, skin or Finger Nails

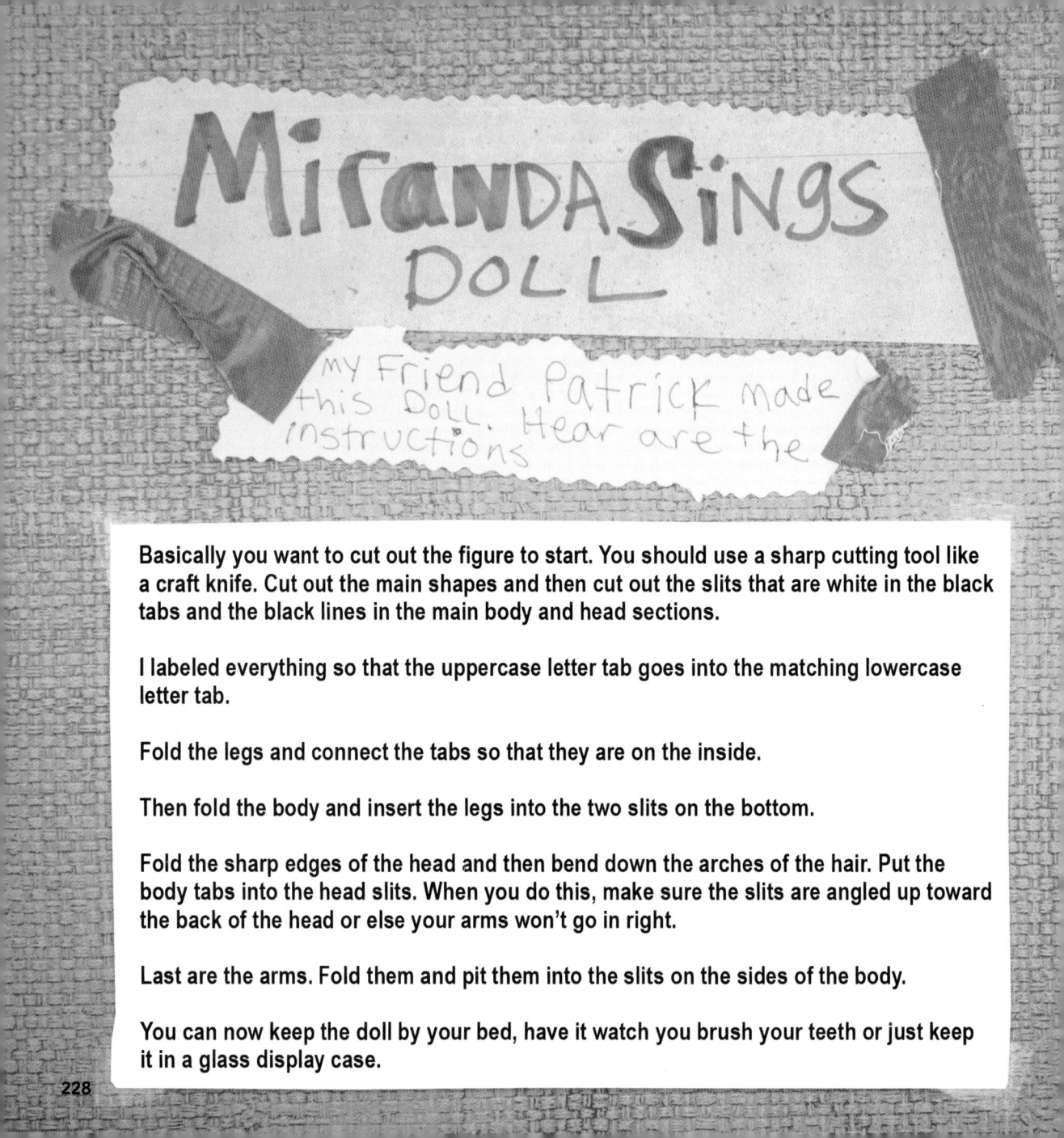

Miranda Sings Doll

My Friend Patrick made this Doll. Hear are the instructions

Basically you want to cut out the figure to start. You should use a sharp cutting tool like a craft knife. Cut out the main shapes and then cut out the slits that are white in the black tabs and the black lines in the main body and head sections.

I labeled everything so that the uppercase letter tab goes into the matching lowercase letter tab.

Fold the legs and connect the tabs so that they are on the inside.

Then fold the body and insert the legs into the two slits on the bottom.

Fold the sharp edges of the head and then bend down the arches of the hair. Put the body tabs into the head slits. When you do this, make sure the slits are angled up toward the back of the head or else your arms won't go in right.

Last are the arms. Fold them and pit them into the slits on the sides of the body.

You can now keep the doll by your bed, have it watch you brush your teeth or just keep it in a glass display case.

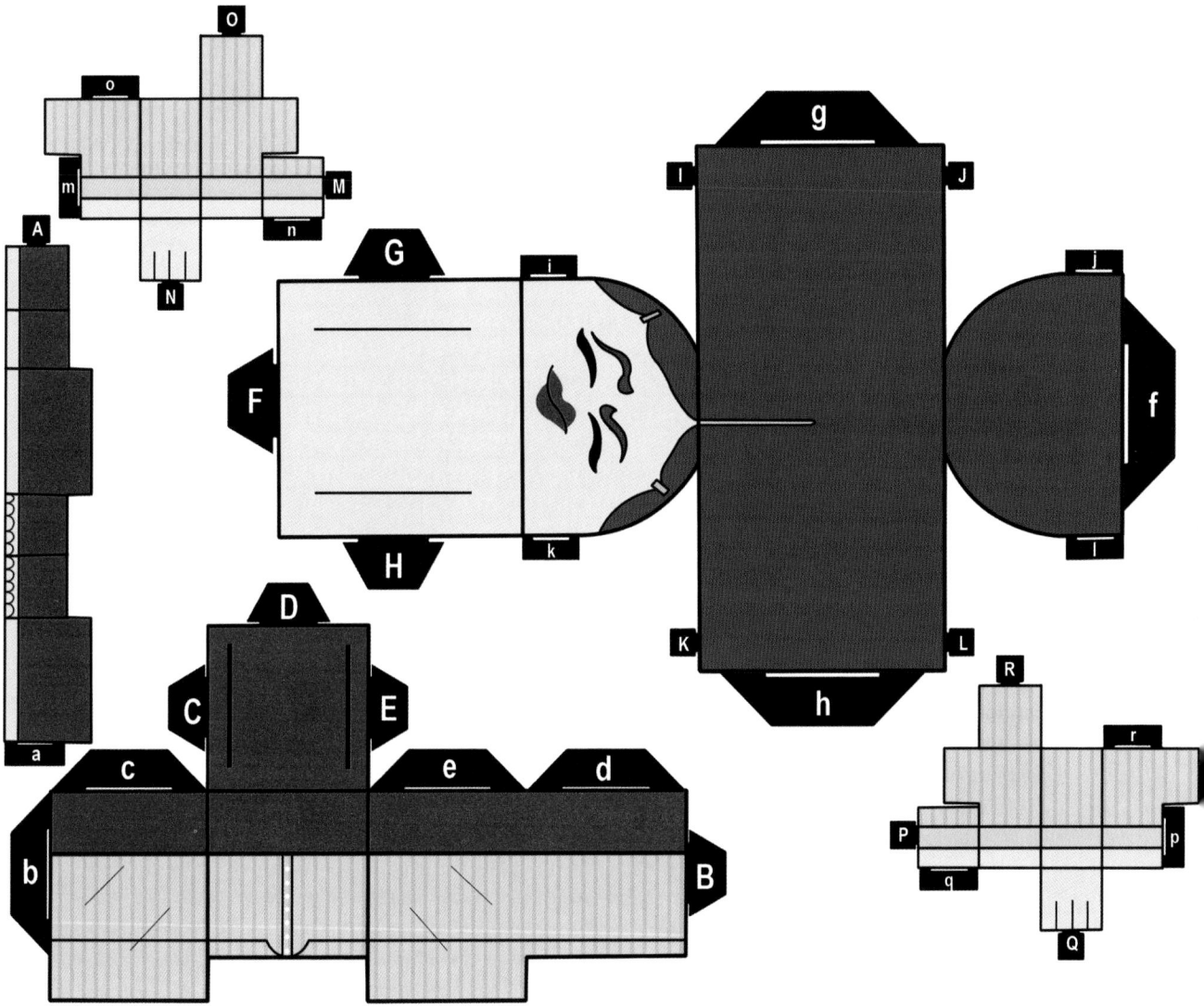
O
o
m
M
n
N
A
a
G
i
F
H
k
g
I
J
j
f
l
K
L
h
D
C
E
c
e
d
b
B
R
r
P
p
q
Q

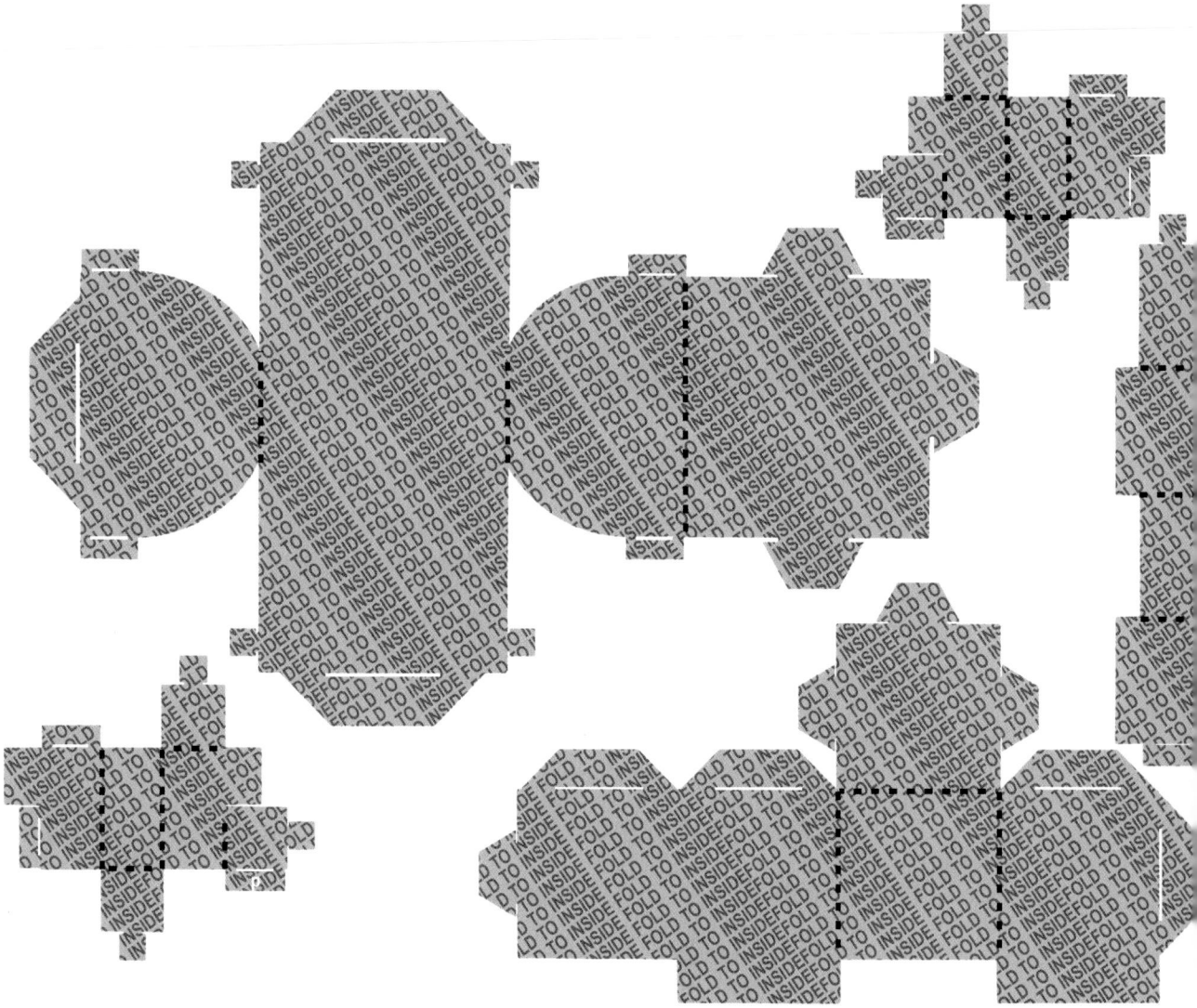
INSIDEFOLD TO INSIDE FOLD

IN CONCLUTCHON

Now that you've red my book, you prabaly r better at everything now. If your not you should get an other copy of my book so you can read it again.

I want to a cours thank all my mirfandas. Also ur welcome for all of the good advice and videos and live shows that i have made for you over the years.

I promice that if you follow all of the laws in my book, you will become a better persen with your love life, your career, you're smarts and most importently your looks. Unless you arent smart or good at things.

also I'm shure that you know some horrible person that needs this book. You should get one for them as a present or tell them that they should by it for themself. That way we can change the world together.

My Diarrhe

is Full of all my Biggest secrets...

DO NOT READ

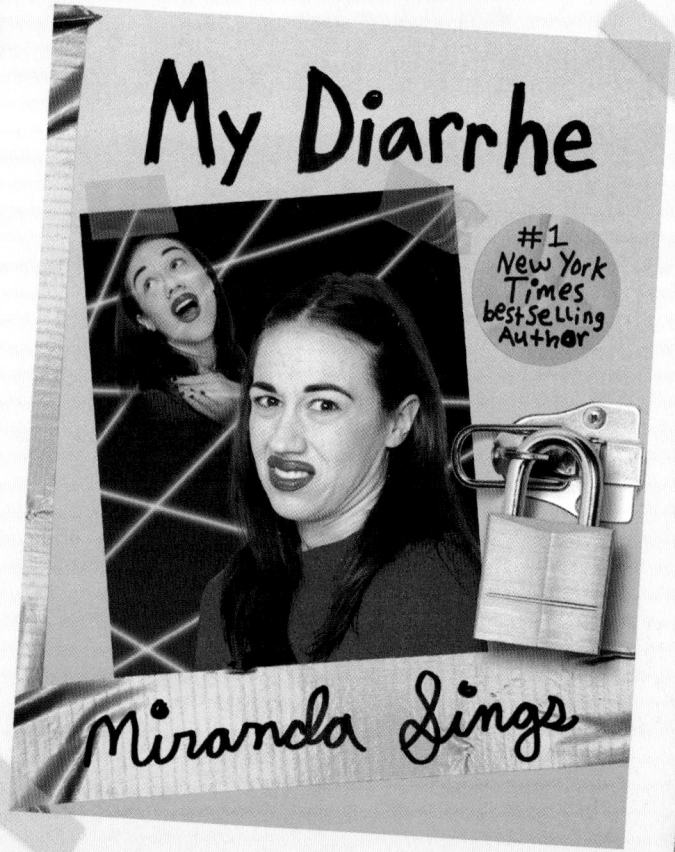

Pick up or download your copy today!

GALLERY BOOKS

66167